AFRICAN ETHNOGRAPHIC STUDIES OF THE 20TH CENTURY

Volume 19

FREEDOM AND AUTHORITY IN FRENCH WEST AFRICA

FREEDOM AND AUTHORITY IN FRENCH WEST AFRICA

ROBERT DELAVIGNETTE

LONDON AND NEW YORK

First published in 1950 by Oxford University Press for the International African Institute, updated in 1968.

This edition first published in 2018
by Routledge
2 Park Square, Milton Park, Abingdon, Oxon OX14 4RN

and by Routledge
711 Third Avenue, New York, NY 10017

Routledge is an imprint of the Taylor & Francis Group, an informa business

© 1950, 1968 International African Institute

All rights reserved. No part of this book may be reprinted or reproduced or utilised in any form or by any electronic, mechanical, or other means, now known or hereafter invented, including photocopying and recording, or in any information storage or retrieval system, without permission in writing from the publishers.

Trademark notice: Product or corporate names may be trademarks or registered trademarks, and are used only for identification and explanation without intent to infringe.

British Library Cataloguing in Publication Data
A catalogue record for this book is available from the British Library

ISBN: 978-0-8153-8713-8 (Set)
ISBN: 978-0-429-48813-9 (Set) (ebk)
ISBN: 978-1-138-57945-3 (Volume 19) (hbk)
ISBN: 978-0-429-50797-7 (Volume 19) (ebk)

Publisher's Note
The publisher has gone to great lengths to ensure the quality of this reprint but points out that some imperfections in the original copies may be apparent.

Disclaimer
The publisher has made every effort to trace copyright holders and would welcome correspondence from those they have been unable to trace.

FREEDOM AND AUTHORITY
IN
FRENCH WEST AFRICA

ROBERT DELAVIGNETTE

Directeur des Affaires Politiques, Ministère de la France d'outre-mer; ancien Directeur de l'Ecole Nationale de la France d'outre-mer.

FRANK CASS & CO. LTD.
1968

First published by Oxford University Press for the
International African Institute

Published by
FRANK CASS AND COMPANY LIMITED
67 Great Russell Street, London WC1
by arrangement

First edition	1950
New impression	1968

A translation of
Service Africain
(Paris, Gallimard, 1946)

The International African Institute desires to
express its thanks to Professor M. Fortes,
Miss Daphne Trevor and Miss M. Manoukian
for the preparation of this translation
which has been edited by its Secretary,
Mrs. B. E. Wyatt.

Printed in Great Britain by
Thomas Nelson (Printers) Ltd., London and Edinburgh

FOREWORD

FIRST of all, I wish to express my thanks to the International African Institute for having undertaken the publication of *Service Africain* in English.[1] To readers of the English version I should like to say what pleasure it gives me to know that *Service Africain* is now presented for their inspection, attention and criticism.

My pleasure is all the greater because never has it been more urgently necessary for the knowledge acquired and the methods tested in Africa by the different European nations to be pooled and compared. Only thus will it be possible or profitable to seek a co-ordination of policies and programmes and in Africa, as in many other parts of the world, it is now very clear that the actions of Britain and France cannot be effective except in so far as they are complementary.

British and French, during the last century, played a vital part in the discovery of Africa and its peoples. Their encounters at the chief crossroads of that continent gave rise to a rivalry which rapidly developed into an emulation profitable to all, and chiefly to the African world.

To-day, if a new stage of progress is to be achieved, experiences, results and proposals must be exchanged, compared and revised. For the discovery of Africa is not all: the task that remains to be done is perhaps more difficult.

On the one hand, it is necessary to take responsibility for its administration, its evolution and, ultimately, its integration into the contemporary world. On the other hand, it is most important to reveal and explain Africa to international opinion which, well-meaning but ill-informed, knows little of it and yet believes it knows enough.

No doubt, we do not envisage our task in the same way. Great Britain is tending towards the formation in Africa of vast negro dominions which to-morrow will be members of a reorganized and expanded Commonwealth. France, on the contrary, faithful to a long tradition, regards her over-sea territories as an integral part of the

---

[1] I would also like to record my debt to an English Africanist, Miss Daphne Trevor, who was responsible for the first draft of the translation.

FOREWORD

national community; she will not, nevertheless, reject the adjustments and adaptations which human and physical conditions overseas demand; but she believes that a wide measure of self-government for local groups will solve the special problems arising in Africa. Paris is not governed in the same way as Lyons, nor Lyons in the same way as Marseilles, but the laws of the Republic are everywhere enforced. This is the direction in which France proposes to advance in order to reconcile her desire to preserve the continuity of the Republic with the legitimate autonomy of African peoples.

But the aim pursued, and in large measure already realized, is the same. Britain and France, by different roads, but to the same extent, have given to the Africans the power to rule themselves. British and French can give an answer to those who, not always with entirely disinterested motives, claim to intervene at the eleventh hour in the government of native territories; we can reply that there are no non-self-governing territories in Africa, only peoples freely associated with the future of Europe.

To introduce native Africa into the modern world; to prepare the world to receive this new continent: these, to-day, are the chief requirements of that service which we are bound to undertake in Africa together until it is completed. May we learn to carry, in fellowship and harmony, this precious but heavy burden.

R. DELAVIGNETTE

Paris: Ministère de la France d'outre-mer.
  Decembre 1949.

CONTENTS

FOREWORD v

I. THE COMMANDANT 7
Functions of the *Cercle*; administration and authority; faith and experiment.

II. COLONIAL SOCIETY 15
Its characteristic qualities; influence of native territories; relation of the Commandant to Colonial Society.

III. THE NATIVE TERRITORIES 34
The indigenous populations; understanding the African territories; the Administration and the native territories; the art of going on tour.

IV. NATIVE POLICY 49
Theories and facts; effects of methods of conquest; Faidherbe and his methods; need for residencies.

V. THE CHIEFS 71
Real Chiefs and substitutes; the canton Chief; the village Chief.

VI. LAW AND CUSTOM 85
The Code and its jurisdiction; customary law; legal status of the village.

VII. THE SPHERE OF THE DIVINE 93
Christianity and native policy; Islam; Fetishism; secular status of the administrator.

VIII. THE PEASANT COMMUNITY 106
Its existence in pre-colonial times; exploitation of the peasantry; relationship of the Commandant to the peasant community; organization of production on a family basis; building up a peasant community.

IX. THE NEW AFRICAN WORLD 139

I. THE COMMANDANT

Administration and Authority
Faith and Experiment

After twenty years in the Colonial Service, I may justly call myself a colonial administrator, and yet I find it increasingly difficult to define what a colonial administrator really is and does. And now that I have to teach the job to my young comrades of the École Nationale de la France d'outre-mer in Paris I find it even harder to formulate than I did when I was actually carrying it out. It used to tax my mind during my days in African residencies, but then it was enough for me to live the life without having to explain it to myself. Now, in Paris, it faces me inescapably within the classroom walls: here you should answer, this you ought to know. Yet the more I think about it, the less I believe that it can be set forth in all its numerous aspects, which vary in importance with different places and times.

In one country, the administrator will be a sort of estate manager; in another, he will be almost entirely a political adviser and mediator; and in a third, where his functions seem to be defined, he will be found some years later transformed into an inspector of export products or a recruiter of labour for State schemes. I tell future colonial administrators that they will have to discover for themselves the particular character of their colony and the appropriate methods of administration. But the words 'colony' and 'administration' do not give an accurate idea of what it is to be a colonial administrator. I try to suggest to the youngsters of the School that they are launching out into a new world which is something other than a colony; that they will not simply be reproducing in the Tropics our European bureaucracy, but practising an art which has within itself a principle of renewal for every administration, in Europe and elsewhere. May I have the power, in training them, to reveal to them this new world of which I am aware and to instil in them a taste for the art which I have served.

It was the physical environment of my first post which brought

2   FREEDOM AND AUTHORITY IN FRENCH WEST AFRICA

home to me the distinctive character of our colonial administration in its most characteristic form—that of a Cercle Commandant.[1] After a short tour at Dakar, and a course at the Colonial School, I was posted to the Niger Territory, and there, though I was stationed at the administrative headquarters and buried in the finance department, I became aware of that agency of government which did not exist at Dakar and was never displayed on the blackboard of the School: the Cercle. Inevitably one's eyes were fixed on it and one was drawn, with the whole population, along the wide track which led to it.

At Zinder there were two towns, the European and the African, or rather the colonial and the native; and between the two, at almost equal distance from each, stood the office of the Cercle, a dwelling unique of its kind.

Our colonial city was lined with symmetrical buildings which served both as offices and residences. Surrounding the Governor's House were the Departments of Economic and Political Affairs, Education, Medicine, Animal Husbandry, Public Works, Posts and Telegraphs, Finance, the Treasury and, a little way off, Army, Ordnance and the barracks, and later, Wireless and Motor Transport. I can see those houses now, built without foundations, looking as if they had been simply dumped there. Their architecture was that of the surrounding cercle: clumsy structures, the apparent solidity of which was belied by their fabric of unbaked bricks. The arched doors and windows were flush with the walls and closed by enormous shutters of palm slats, called seccos, fastened by a peg in the middle. The only means of ventilation was to raise or lower this corrugated screen, which was often torn off by tornadoes in the rainy season, and in the dry weather by the east wind.

The Cercle had the same outer shell as we had, the same flat roofs, the same lanes of cactus and thornbush baked under the same sun. But the Cercle lived a life of its own, at a deeper level than ours, its rhythm directly at grips with the country.

The first thing that struck one was its rural air. Our ration of water for drinking, cooking, showers, washing-up, laundering, was brought round to us by the Cercle oxen. It was to the Cercle that our cooks went in quest of meat, vegetables, eggs and firewood, for it dominated the market. The Cercle alone communicated with the oasis, where gardens flourished among the canals and wells. For everything which

---

[1] Translator's note: It has been thought advisable not to attempt a translation of this term since no one exact equivalent exists in British Colonial practice.

THE COMMANDANT

concerned our domestic life it attached us to that African soil where our untrained eyes would have been lost in a wilderness of grassland that bore no crops and trees without fruit.

Into our task of administration it brought the ideal of a real world. Working in the Finance Department I checked the bills for transport: 'Owing to Hamani, cameleer, for supplying 3 camels for 14 days, from Zinder to Agades, 1 fr. 50 per day per animal.' But it was with the camels and their master Hamani in flesh and blood, with Africa in the raw, that the *Cercle* lived and had its being. Twice a year it gathered hundreds of animals and men on the steps of its veranda for the great caravan from Agades and Bilma, and in the apt pidgin French phrase 'leur donnait la route', the road of the desert post, the harshest and most alluring of them all. Indeed at all times it was like a ship-yard compared with us on our office stools, a round of activity beside our routine of paperwork. Its island position between the two towns made it the more conspicuous.

I dreamed that the *Cercle* might 'give me the road' of the great highways which crossed the territory—seventy-five days' trek from Niamey to N'Guigmi and ninety-eight from Gaya to Bardai—or simply that it might show me the paths to the villages where things were grown, and to the walled towns, or perhaps take me with the flocks moving to new pastures, the pedlars on their slow rounds or the pilgrims in their tribulations. Shut in as I was with the Dahomean copying clerks, I tried through them to traffic in African life in a small way since I was barred from the large-scale activities of the *Cercle*. But the clerks, with their ebony faces gleaming like well-polished office furniture, were better bureaucrats than I was. They taught me how to check the colony's accounts rather than how to get to know the Africa of Zinder, which was not their native home and where they lived as expatriates. Their names—Sacramento, Pinto, Silva, Medeiros—names of old Portuguese slavers—were reminders of that fearful traffic, but they also recalled the earlier contact with the natives which, inhuman as it might have been, was not impersonal. In the gusts of the east wind that fluttered the pages of our account books I felt the breath of Africa. It got me down, but it whipped the *Cercle* up into greater activity. And it seemed to me that if only I could work at the *Cercle* I would get the smell of the country.

The natives in our city, the colonial city, were guards and orderlies, cooks and their scullions, boys with their 'small boys' who worked the punkahs; and women for our need, prostitutes for a night, or

4 FREEDOM AND AUTHORITY IN FRENCH WEST AFRICA

concubines for a tour,[1] sometimes servant-mistresses for a lifetime. For the threescore of us Europeans, there were about three hundred servants; a mysterious company, who did what they had to do without bringing us any real contact with the neighbouring world from which they came. And, though they lived with their families in restricted quarters in our buildings, they would slip out at times to recapture in the native city the life which they lacked among us. With a shuffle of naked feet—so different from the step of any European—they would disappear in response to some cry from a mosque, some rumour of the market-place or beat of the drums, or even, it seemed, drawn by some silence; whatever it may have been, the *Cercle* knew all about it.

The native city presented a dual aspect; it comprised the 'Zengou' or commercial quarter, and the 'Birni', a feudal stronghold. The former spread out its stalls and caravans in a dusty bowl, the other, on rising ground bristling with craggy weatherbeaten rocks, enclosed in a ruin of bare and crumbling brickwork the Sultan and his court.

In this dual city lived ten thousand souls. The life there had a reality and a quality which, surprising and alien though it might be, was yet unmistakably its own. The people did not speak pidgin, but their own languages: the Tamshek of the Aïr caravan-men, the Fulfulde of the herdsmen and overlords; the Arabic used by the faithful for public prayer and by the literates for writing; the Djerma of the troops from Dosso; and, main theme of the symphony, the Hausa of the peasants and the pedlars. The very word Zinder which we used as an administrative term, was changed on the lips of the town into a real name: Damagaram.

The peasants (*talakkas*) were barely emancipated serfs and bent the knee to their masters the nobles (*zarkis*). Deportment and speech were graced with formal courtesy expressed in phrases which, varying with the occasion, had remained unchanged since time began. 'How-goes-it-this-morning'—'How-goes-it-this-evening', 'How is it with the house', concluding with a chant 'Peace—everywhere peace', hymned by men who hid knives under their leather jerkins, when they did not lean on lances or carry broadswords slung at their sides or daggers in their armpits. And these weapons did not seem anachronisms. They glinted in the alley-ways, in the market-place, in the vaulted rooms of the Sultan.

---

[1] Translator's note: The administrator's term in the colony between leaves, usually eighteen months; also, of course, a tour through the administrator's district. The word is used in both senses in the British Colonial Service as well.

THE COMMANDANT 5

In the hollow inner courtyards of the *Birni*, in the elbow-turn of passages, in ante-rooms under domed or vaulted ceilings where the ground was covered with squatting men, heel-less slippers and dung, gathered the landowners of the cantons, pilgrims from Mecca, merchants from Kano and even from Tripoli, who came to pay ceremonial visits to the Sultan, the 'Zarki of Zarkis'. Barma Mata, 'Zarki n'Damagaram', his head sunk in blouses stiff with indigo, received them sitting on the ceremonial bed in a low-ceilinged room thick with incense, wearing the air of a caged beast, though no longer wild. He was made Sultan by the French, and now he watched and waited perhaps for the improbable return of his ancient power, forgetting his vigilant neighbour, set between the native city and the colonial city: the *Cercle*. A neighbour with a relentless memory, who knew the story of Captain Casemajor and the interpreter Olive, assassinated in 1898; who knew how the former Sultan had been deposed and Barma Mata put in his place and made to toe the line. There was no one in the *Birni*, no fanatical shoemaker attached to the Senussi fraternities of the desert, no one in the *Zengou* or the cantons, there was not a man who did not hear and obey when the *Cercle*, using the greeting of the country, said: 'Peace—everywhere peace'.

This was no fantastic pageant unfolding itself before me, but political authority expressed with complete confidence. The *Cercle* governed 10,000 souls in the town and 135,000 in the cantons. In the Niger territory, an area more than half as large as France, with a population of one million, there were 27 *cercles* with 21 administrators and 39 officers for native affairs, in all 60 government officials. In French West Africa, an area eight times the size of France, with a population of fifteen million, there were 118 *cercles*. In Senegal, Guinea, the Ivory Coast, Dahomey, Mauretania, in Upper Senegal, Upper Volta and our own territory of the Niger, the basic administrative unit was the *Cercle*. By its edict it ensured peace. In that melting-pot of populations, ranging from bronze to copper colour, it did not manufacture slavish robots, but tested out the human motives which maintain peace. The skin texture, the voice-inflection of these Fulani and Hamites were expressions of a reality unknown to government departments; but for the *Cercle* this was the normal colour, this the very fibre and speech of humanity: this was the family which had to be kept in peace.

The *Cercle* carried out a real policy: that is to say, it did not confine itself to keeping watch over the petty intrigues of the *zarkis*. Damagaram—not only the town but the cantons, the valleys of poor soil,

6   FREEDOM AND AUTHORITY IN FRENCH WEST AFRICA

the bush with its scanty pasture, the whole meagre rural economy with its faint movement of life in the fields and villages, where wide spaces, ravaged and lifeless, were a constant reminder, to the unresisting natives and the incredulous colonials alike, of the proximity of the desert and its lunar death—all this was no mere decorative background but the social setting for the manifold activities of the *Cercle*. Innumerable stubborn tasks, small in themselves but magnified by the hostility of the desert, had to be undertaken to preserve the land of Damaragam for Africa, and for an Africa no longer cut off from the world as in the past, but entering as a partner into a new world. And I used to ask myself: How does the *Cercle* tackle it?

I saw the officers of the *Cercle*, with their interpreters and guards, presiding at courts, holding palavers, going on tour. But how did their administration work? Like us, they had their files and wrote reports. But it was not the same thing, and there was something more to it. Judgments were given on the basis of the Digest of Colonial Law Regulations, yet they seemed to have been thought out by the indigenous mind of the country. Tax was collected on the basis of the figures of the administration's Budget, which was drawn up in our Finance Department, typed by our Dahomeans and printed by the Dakar Government printer; but behind this Budget the *Cercle* had counted the sous, the crowns, the dirty notes folded lengthwise in the native manner; it had estimated the revenue from fields and flocks, the profits of trading corporations, from butchers to herbalists. It was all far from perfect, distressingly rough and ready; but how did the *Cercle* get the spirit of the taxed into its taxes, the spirit of those judged into its justice? The *Cercle* had eyes and ears: it was aware of a significance in the life of the people which eluded our world of papers. How could one acquire that flair, so that in the act of administering justice or levying tax one could remain a living person?

The man who really personified the *Cercle* was the Commandant, and he was not a civil servant like us. He was not a specialist in any branch of administration, nor was he lost in an academic theory of administration in general. He was the Chief of a clearly defined country called Damaragam, and Chief in everything that concerned that country. At that time the Commandant was Henry Fleury, a man of some forty years of age, who had begun as a clerk in Dakar in 1902. Twenty years later he was only a first-grade Deputy Administrator. Most of the Zinder bureaucrats were of higher rank. But his position was independent of all ranks and he maintained it successfully. Tall, though appearing shortish on horseback, alert though corpulent,

THE COMMANDANT

with a high colour under the mane of his beard, a big nose, eyes flaming behind his spectacles, he led an extremely active life. His only material privilege was separate living quarters. Even when he was in Zinder, he did not look like a townsman. He conducted himself at Zinder as he had done at his previous posts in the bush—Bamba, Bourem, Tillabéry. He kept his tool-box with him; he had no need to unpack it, but it reminded him of the wild solitudes in which he had enjoyed prising open the provision cases so that he could use the wood. He carried a knife in his pocket like a peasant, though he was born in Paris. Unlike the civil servants at Headquarters, who were to the natives merely the Europeans of Zinder, and sometimes the white man of this or that department—Finance or Telegraphs—he had his own special nickname: 'Thief-Purger.' And it was not only in court that he purged the country of its rogues and vagabonds, but on tour, when he would give a good dressing-down in private to the *zarki* who was cheating the villages over tax-money. This was his way also with certain colonials who traded secretly in coin and cattle.

He had a seat at the Governor's weekly conference of department heads, and he was listened to as long as the Governor was M. Brévié, who thought very highly of him. I imagine he went there with the same brusque manner which he used with the Sultan, and that he would create one of those silences where the angel of truth passes overhead. Thief-Purger knew how to show them the miserable state of Damagaram, where the *zarkis* pillaged the *talakkas*, and where the Commissariat and a bureaucratic administration drained the country by their exactions. Himself at grips with people and regulations, he had his own rules. He was never taken in by official impostures. For example, if he had to make a payment to an illiterate African, he obeyed the regulation which required two literate witnesses and their signatures; but since it was always the same two witnesses, he also demanded what so many administrators, content with the formality of the signatures, forgot, namely, that the man to be paid should actually be there and get his money. He kept a watch, and a sharp watch, on these little precautions. He didn't juggle with statistics, and he didn't easily agree to let planning enthusiasts have an extra sou added to the poll-tax or an extra mile of road to the labour service projects. He didn't trust ideas from headquarters, whether headquarters was Zinder, Dakar or Paris. And he would willingly have copied that Commandant of the Mossi *Cercle* who stuck departmental circulars in his trouser-pockets before he had read them so as to have them handy when he had a free moment, but

8   FREEDOM AND AUTHORITY IN FRENCH WEST AFRICA

in the evening threw his trousers, soaked in the sweat of a day's work, into the dirty-linen basket, and the circulars with them. Henry Fleury also got his trousers soaked in sweat, often from travelling into distant cantons where an epidemic or a famine was raging. Even when there was nothing or not much that he could do, he went to see. When he came back, his temper was not of the best. As Commandant of Zinder *Cercle*, his job was to protect Damagaram, without having any illusions about the people, whether *zarkis* or *talakkas*. When his anger was aroused against the people or against our officials, he would pull furiously at his empty pipe as he thought of the swarms of lice and locusts which were destroying the villages by typhus or starvation, and would make a determined stand, alone and dominating. I learned from him that even to keep a country going, a Commandant has to wage war on two fronts, against the natives and against the officials, and he does not deal his blows with palavers or reports.

When I, in my turn, was flung into territorial administration, I experienced a difficulty which still troubles me. The first time I was able to step back and see the colony in perspective, that is, on my first leave, I found it was not easy to explain what I had been doing. If I told French people in Europe of all the different things I had to do in the same job and even on the same day, they did not understand that all these made up one job, and that in going from the courts to a road-making project, from road-making to a census, from a census to agriculture—from one task to another, I was not changing my job; or else they thought: This colony is only a black man's country and does not require a highly developed government if one man can do everything. They did not recognize the revolution in administrative method which this meant, or the new world it had produced. They did not suspect that the colony was no longer a strange and alien realm but an integral part of the modern world with a vigorous native life. And this local development, no less than the world situation, demanded, not officials of the old-fashioned European type, strictly specialized as to their functions, but Chiefs, in whose hands all essential duties could be concentrated, who would be concerned sometimes with law, sometimes with roads, and always with the future. The colonial administrator was playing a leading part in the building of a world just because he was a man of all work in his own corner of it, and, as he watched the Africans there growing into full manhood, he was translating into fact with them the hope of a new world.

Perhaps it was the circumstances of my first departure for the colony that sent me chasing the vision of a new world. I left metropolitan France on the morrow of the war of 1914–18. War still covered its soil with ruins. In that bulge in the Champagne front which had become a district of the Liberated Areas, my father was rebuilding his factory. The little country town, like thousands of others, had to be raised up again, roads and farms, church, school, town hall; and Rheims, just nearby, with its scarred cathedral, towered over one of the greatest charnel-houses but also one of the greatest housing schemes in recorded history. Piedmontese cement-workers, Annamite and Berber labourers, and German prisoners of war, lived all around us in encampments still camouflaged in their cunning and primitive war-paint. Into the gas-lit hutments stored with tinned food swarmed a leather-jacketed tribe. One would have thought oneself at the founding of some America were it not for that apocalyptic scrap-iron and those plantations of wooden crosses. We burned splintered beams in the fire-place to fight the cold sweat on the walls that brought to mind the wretched dead in their damp graves. My father did not know where to begin amid the ruins to get the plan of the factory going. Never did an emigrant leave his home in so desolate a mess as the son who went off thinking on a sudden that his parents showed more courage in staying to rebuild France than he did in speeding towards colonial skies.

I also had landed myself in a country where villages were waiting to be rebuilt and towns waiting to be planned. The father in the liberated regions of Champagne, the son in those of the Niger, exchanged news of their work. I looked at photos of the factory which was taking shape and of my father standing on the new sky-line of reinforced concrete roofs. He in his turn saw me in the sweltering bush leading a gang to collect palmwood for building the Residency. But it was not made sufficiently clear to us that our task was to build a new world. Metropolitan France, though bled by the war, did not lack credit, machines or workers. Yet the work was not the pioneering it should have been. It encountered an old world that brought out ghosts from the background to house them in the new dwellings. My father grew old rebuilding a factory where he could not introduce the new organization he had in mind. The factory was enlarged, and somewhat improved technically, but it retained the old defects of economic and social structure. The so-called liberated areas were not freed from administrative routine. In place of a new organization, the old departmental structure was patched up. France in Africa had no money or technical equipment, and its workers were yesterday's

10 FREEDOM AND AUTHORITY IN FRENCH WEST AFRICA

slaves now doing labour service. But on the Niger the new world emergent could be distinguished more clearly than in Champagne. And there, paying for it in my person, I absorbed a belief in the necessity of exercising authority. When I went back to metropolitan France, the very place where people thought they were doing something new in a big way, everything smelt stale and felt cramped. The fault lay with an impersonal, irresponsible, routine-ridden administration. There was no Command. In Africa, on the contrary, poverty-stricken as we were, we were experimenting with the administration of the future, the administration which will bring together humanism and authority. We were preserving that function of authority in which resides the vital spirit of the new world. Our activities extended beyond the colony and our method of administration affected whites as well as blacks. This is beginning to become apparent in the economic sphere. If the groundnuts of Senegal give us oil and soap, if bananas from Guinea appear in our village shops or on barrows in the streets of Paris, it is because, somewhere in Africa, at Kaolack or Kindia, there is a Commandant. He is not merely an official at some distant outpost; he controls a new force in the area he administers; not only does he send to the French in Europe the luxuries to which they have become accustomed without knowing much about their origin or their cost in terms of human activity, but he also transmits a sort of energy, of whose nature they know nothing though they are vaguely aware of the need for it.

How often, in a Soudanese settlement, alone with the life which breathes in a wretched huddle of native huts scarcely distinguishable from the surrounding bush, have I thought that the colonial administrator is the unknown electrician in the power house of a new order of life, just as much for Africa as for France. It is a question of releasing the powers of Europe and Africa and transforming them into socially valuable forces. The commandant of the *Cercle* smiles in his solitude when he makes contact with that electricity.

Henry Fleury, Thief-Purger, Commandant at Zinder, one of the eighteen *cercles* of French West Africa, taught me by his example that the colonial administrator does not fill an administrative position in the colonies, but exercises direct authority in a real country. The natives make no mistake about it—they call him Commandant, naming him by his primary function, his essential activity. He commands effectively only if his whole personality is engaged. And the way he commands, though it is in the heart of Africa, affects not only the natives, and involves not only himself, but Europeans as well. This

THE COMMANDANT

is little enough realized, still less correctly understood. It is often supposed that colonial command reflects a feudal spirit, or that it represents a summary form of administration which will progress by differentiation of functions, and so shed its character of personal authority. No, this command is as independent of the Africa of estate-owners as it is of the Europe of civil servants. It is not feudalism, nor bureaucracy, but a territorial administration. And it is the only humane form of government in Africa, Europe or anywhere else, because it is the only one where those who govern see those who are governed as living men. And when this system appears harsh, or, on the contrary, powerless, it is because it has been rendered sterile by a so-called higher administration, which has lost all human feeling in a pedantry of regulations.

There is no administrative problem, however well-conceived the departmental instructions on it, which does not change its nature when it comes down to earth somewhere. And that somewhere is a country with depth as well as extension. The administrative problem immediately raises a native problem, that is to say a human problem, which demands a solution not only according to the regulations but in the moral sphere. This at once brings into play the necessity for authority. A road to map out, a population to vaccinate, a school to open—just so many local and native questions; and the administrator, who is perfectly well aware that the country cannot be run by written reports, looks for men, the men he has to command in order to get this particular thing done. Even if he has the help of specialists, as they are called in Europe, the engineer, the doctor and the teacher will in turn need his knowledge of the country and his authority. They will need them in order to get the roadmakers on the road, and— surprising as it may seem—to get the patients into the hospitals and the children into the schools. They would face only an inert mass if the people of the country were not revealed to them. And the natives, on their side, hold back and wait for the administrator to show them the way and set them on the road to the new world where the African rides in a car, vaccinates his children against smallpox and has them taught French. This is a human problem which the administrator cannot solve by making humanitarian or authoritarian statements, but only by sounding the note of authority with the precision of the humanist.

A feature of territorial colonial administration is its positive humanity, which wears an air of revolutionary authority. The territorial colonial administration is charged with introducing a new

12 FREEDOM AND AUTHORITY IN FRENCH WEST AFRICA

political and economic régime into the country: it is concentrated in the hands of a few Europeans who can only communicate through intermediaries with the masses they govern, and from whom they are separated by ways of life, forms of thought and methods of work. How could this administration be anything but revolutionary and authoritarian? To contest this is to be afraid of words and hypocritically to leave the way open for a parade-ground militarism, a caricature of military command. On the contrary, in order to humanize this authority, it is necessary to bring it into the light and entrust it to responsible people. There is an inner principle proper to territorial colonial administration: the personal authority of the administrator and, in the final analysis, his personal character expressed in the exercise of authority.

Nowadays we go to Africa by plane, with maps which show the progress of our knowledge: the coastline is accurately drawn, rivers and mountains are sited and measured, the soil is surveyed. But on our mental journeys we still seem to carry with us in our baggage the old clichés of our ancestors: the Africans are good-hearted savages, or inferior men, or again, only big children. However, during the last few years we have begun to study them as they are in their own Africa and not as we have classified them in conventional categories. But in exploring their ethnology and sociology we are in danger of losing sight of the importance of administration, as if the art of administering them as men of Africa and citizens of the world were merely a mechanism wound up once for all in government offices. The old maps are no longer applied to the natives, but they still are to the Colonials. Credit is taken for knowing the natives, while the social importance of the administrative structure—which indeed the natives are breaking down as they develop—is neglected. This structure is dismissed as useless, but it is not realized that African societies would fall to pieces if they were not worked into it; or else it is considered good enough as it is, and the administrative policy consists in furbishing up the old framework.

Your anthropologist will establish a classification of lip plugs among the Bobo—those splinters of bone, quartz, copper or glass that the people, especially the women, wear in their lower lips—and yet take no interest in that art which has opened up the Bobo country to the other Africas and the play of world forces. He will go by car from village to village looking for lip plugs, on the road built by the *Cercle* Commandant, and never ask how he made it and how he organized his human material for the making of the road. The truth

THE COMMANDANT

is, the indigenous societies can no longer be studied apart from the territorial administration; nor can the country be understood without some notion of the art of government in the *Cercle*, however difficult that art may be to grasp from outside.

With the inter-dependence of Africa and Europe, this art is being infected with European bureaucracy and is becoming less intelligible to its own practitioners. The administrator on tour in a village of straw huts may smile in his isolation and think that Africa has the status of a colony, and as a colony makes its impression on Europe, but that very few, either black or white, have any clear idea of the art which he practises. This is perhaps why he feels isolated. He may fear that Europe will commit suicide to-morrow in a conflagration due to some colonial question, through failure to understand what it means to administer a bush village. So he comes to think of his job as a dangerous one, though not in the same way as in the past. It is no longer the lion prowling round the camp, but the primitive ignorance of Europe which beleaguers the colony and its administration. A territory has to be administered, and, in order to administer, it is necessary to exercise authority. It is not a matter of aping the ways of the barrack square, parading about with guards, insisting on salutes and processions, or interpreting regulations with hair-splitting subtlety, but of believing and acting. It is a question of faith and method.

Faith in the human value of the natives, even if—particularly if— they are reputed savages, and faith in the new world which will be built with them. They will enter the new world of the colony as men, and not as subjects; the colony will only live in so far as they infuse their own life into it by renewing their own country. And just because their administrator measures the difference between their mentality and his, he seeks methodically to get to know them as men, to regulate his authority over them, co-operating with their councils of notables and workers in the task he is carrying out with them.

Methods exist. For fifty years administrators have been on the job in the *Cercles* and we can hammer out what is to be learnt from their efforts. We can contrast our new methods with the old idea that colonial government consisted of an ideology at the top and militarism below. These methods are experimental. The plural is used simply to make it clear that there is no single golden rule. The administrator in his work must preserve the intellectual integrity of the scientist conducting an experiment. He observes and checks his action by its effect on the country and the country's reaction to it. Perhaps a road

14 FREEDOM AND AUTHORITY IN FRENCH WEST AFRICA

is to be constructed by labour service, which is a dangerous weapon and may turn into forced labour if badly administered. The administrator tries out on the territory the labour service regulations and the Public Works engineer's plan. He organizes native labour on the road as a function of the people of the country and takes note of their efforts. If he finds the working-day going with a swing, shifts relieving each other efficiently, if he succeeds in harmonizing the collective effort which he imposes, then he will have brought into the toilsome *corvée* of poor people, clearing and levelling and ditching with poor tools, the spirit of an experiment honestly carried out. And if he can manage it so that the people stay at work on the road, he is more than a road-builder, he is a true Commander.

The discipline of the experimental method does not exclude personal character in command. There are never cut-and-dried solutions. There is the territory and there is the administrator, who knows the regulations well enough to re-think them in terms of the place where the experiment has to be tried out, who digs down constantly into the country's inexhaustible fund of human experience and thereby enriches his own character and the relationship between the work he does and the free spirit that must remain his.

II. COLONIAL SOCIETY

Its Characteristic Qualities

It is European

THE Commandant must understand Colonial Society, for it is always with him. The smallest *cercle* in the bush numbers at least a few Europeans, enough to embody Colonial Society. Even if the Commandant were completely alone, he would still be responsible to a headquarters where Colonial Society rules.

Its primary characteristic is that it is European, as is evident as soon as one lands at Dakar. Nothing strikes the new-comer more forcibly than the way this European quality meets the eye, even among the crowds gathered at the quayside. The young Colonial is confronted by Europe, in starched white summer clothes, standing out in high relief against the African background. He quickly becomes part of it, and goes everywhere, even to mass and to communion, as a member of this society.

On the wooden building which, in 1920, overlooked the harbour at Dakar, flashed the word 'Europe', a symbol, as it were, of colonial solidarity; this was the 'Hôtel de l'Europe', and it was under the flag of Europe that I took my first meals in Senegal.

In 1934, on the fiftieth anniversary of the Soudan,[1] the old Soudanese, that is to say the soldiers of the conquest of the Soudan, Generals Peltier, Meynier, Quiquandon, Gouraud, and the great Binger himself, men who had Africa in their blood, were greeted at every turn as they passed together through the streets of Bamako or along the Segou quay by the great shout of the natives: 'The Europeans, there are the Europeans.' Some of them had led the African army into the trenches against the Hindenburg line in Champagne during the world war of 1914–18. Back in the Soudan of their youth, they were still nevertheless 'the Europeans'.

That Colonial Society should be European is a more curious matter than it looks, and calls for an explanation. It was on the eve

---

[1] Translator's note: I have kept the French spelling to avoid confusion with the Anglo-Egyptian Sudan.

16   FREEDOM AND AUTHORITY IN FRENCH WEST AFRICA

of the great African explorations that Europe split in two: on the one hand the Europe of the French Revolution, on the other the Europe of the *ancien régime*. At the moment when it discovered the Black Continent, it lost its own unity. Nevertheless in opening up Africa to the world, it acted as a universal civilization, rather than as any national imperialism. 'Civilization' was the new word that all Europe in the nineteenth century was pronouncing with fervour, and to which it gave one meaning. It got into the Dictionary of the French Academy in 1835, at the very moment when the Royal Geographical Societies were bending their thoughts towards mysterious Timbuctoo. When European explorers spoke of civilizing Africa they were really united in a common sentiment and logic, in which the romance of discovery joined hands with the positivism of organization. Threats of war might flare up in Europe on the subject of dividing Africa; they proclaimed the importance of the word European as much as the superiority of one European nation over another. Admittedly, later on, English and French vied with each other for Ouagadougou or clashed at Fashoda; but at the same time they were both Europeans, rival champions of the same cause. In savanna and forest they carried on a race towards civilization, not a conflict between civilizations. They played the game by rules drawn up at Berlin in 1885 in a conference of national delegates directed by the Prussian Bismarck. They agreed on certain fundamental principles and certain essential practices which they called Civilization with a capital C.

This game was played in the dense forests, the scrub-covered savannas, the curdled desert—the three geographical stories of the old African home in the sun. The English, the French, and in a sense, the Portuguese, and later the Belgians, the Italians and the Germans themselves, competed against each other, not like pontiffs of hostile sects, but like runners, to see who would win through first to river or town, who would mark the greatest number of points on the map. In Europe they were already out of tune, bristling with conscript soldiers, ruining themselves with armaments. Africa, on the contrary, endowed them with an astonishing unity. In this exotic setting, the European emerged in his true nature. Whatever his nationality, he wore the same helmet, the same white or khaki uniform; he displayed the same faith in Civilization, he bore the same burden of creating new Europes. He had the same reactions towards the native countries, which were to him a building site.

Barth, the German, who explored the Soudan where, some years after he had passed through, Italy was to acquire Tripoli, England

Kano and France Timbuctoo, was a European; so was the American Stanley who found the Englishman Livingstone in the Congo and gave him news of the Franco-Prussian War of 1870 and the Paris Commune.

And the Europe of the Revolution and that of the *ancien régime*, far from fighting each other in Africa, worked together on the same task. The young cavalry officer, De la Tour Saint-Ygest, who perhaps left France because he could not stand the revolutionary equality there, went off to Upper Senegal-Niger to destroy the feudal power of the Tuareg, the principles and sentiments of which he cherished. On the other hand, the man who wielded the power of the Republic at Dakar, adherent of a French Freemason lodge, and member of the Radical-Socialist party, was to become in Africa a governor fanatically attached to old-style hierarchy, using autocratic methods to lead the natives along the path of progress.

Thus European civilization has been served in Africa by very diverse and hostile nations, and by men within one nation as different as a baron of the *ancien régime* and a Republican civil servant. This civilization holds as an axiom man's sovereignty over nature, and endorses in Africa as in Europe and throughout the world, Buffon's declaration: 'Man can and must attempt all.' Man must put the world in order. This determination has the compelling power of a religion, and the European is its prophet. From subaltern to Governor-General Colonial Society is European in its reverence for Progress —what it calls Progress—in its pride at leading the march of progress and controlling its instruments: the rifle no less than the railway, the share market as well as the decree of the Council of State.

It is a minority. It is national and provincial

It is very clear indeed that Colonial Society in Africa is everywhere an extremely small minority. In French West Africa there are 28,000[1] Europeans at the most as against fifteen million natives.

The proportion of Europeans to natives in tropical Africa is as follows:

Union of South Africa	250 per thousand
Former German S.W. Africa[2]	100 ,,
Rhodesia	45 ,,

[1] 27,331 in 1933; 24,798 in 1938, made up as follows: 3,041 soldiers, 6,200 women, 4,300 children.

[2] Before the 1914–18 War, German colonies showed the following proportion: Europeans, 22,405; natives, 11,406,000. Of these 22,405 Europeans, 14,800 were concentrated in German S.W. Africa among 79,556 natives.

18   FREEDOM AND AUTHORITY IN FRENCH WEST AFRICA

Angola	10	,,
Kenya	5	,,
Belgian Congo	2	,,
French and British West Africa and French Equatorial Africa	1	,,

Turning to the percentage of European officials in relation to the native population one has a still more striking index of the minority character of Colonial Society:

	European Officials	*Native Population*
British Nigeria	1,315	20,000,000
Belgian Congo	2,384	9,400,000
French Equatorial Africa	887	3,200,000
French West Africa	3,660[1]	15,000,000

Another aspect of this minority character is the proportion of colonials in relation to their home country: less than one per thousand.

When I say that Colonial Society is national, I mean that it mirrors its home country; it is European without being a mosaic of different European nationalities. It is composed mainly of Englishmen in the English colonies, of French in the French colonies. There is nevertheless a fairly high proportion of foreigners;[2] thus in the French Cameroons in 1938 there were 3,000 Europeans (as against over $2\frac{1}{4}$ million natives) of whom more than 800 were foreigners.[3] In French West Africa, 7,650 foreigners; but there you have a special case, the Syrians and Lebanese, who almost monopolize the retail trade as middlemen between the big European firms and the natives. Numbering 6,235, they are counted among the 28,000 members of Colonial Society in French West Africa; but whether they are socially merged with it, whether they lead in Africa, particularly in Senegal and Guinea where most of them live, a European way of life is another question.

Colonial Society in the different colonies in Africa is self-sufficient and very set in its ways. It is only inter-colonial at Vichy where its members nurse their livers and chance upon, rather than frequent the company of, their Asiatic or Madagascan equivalents. It is not international, though sometimes it discovers in other Colonial Societies

---

[1] In 1908 there were only 1,200. But those were the days when 6,000 villages and two million men in the Mossi country were administered by ten Europeans.

[2] E.g. Belgian Congo in 1938, 23,091 Europeans, of whom a third are non-Belgians. This proportion has remained constant since 1930.

[3] 2,161 French, 148 Greeks, 108 Americans, 105 Germans, 99 Swiss, 85 English, 66 Lebanese, 49 Italians, 40 Spaniards, 28 Belgians, 16 Norwegians, 10 Canadians, 20 Portuguese; 20 Czechoslovaks, 5 Dutch.

COLONIAL SOCIETY

kindred customs and cultural affinities which lead it to the notion of a United Europe, a 'White' empire, founded by statute upon 740 million coloured people.

The French colonial of Africa sees liners at Dakar, the finest of which serve the South American lines. Rio de Janeiro is no further from him than Bordeaux or Cotonou. But he has no curiosity about Brazil. A few hours by car from his post he has an English neighbour, but he won't go and see him (though he may read Kipling, which the Englishman probably no longer does). The fact is that colonial life is burdensome and busy. It teaches one not to entertain curiosity about the wide world. A corner of Africa to get to the bottom of, to work in and on, is enough to absorb one entirely. The rest is superficial cosmopolitanism. One sets up house with Africa: a 'marriage of reason' in which one is too tired to be unfaithful. In the beginning was the voyage—a honeymoon memory. Living together afterwards, one no longer travels, except on tour in Africa itself. One spends one's leave in France, or sometimes travelling as a tourist elsewhere in Europe. One does one's tour in Africa. And between tour and leave there is the crossing—which is no longer the voyage it was the first time; the colonial rarely remains the traveller, the new man that awoke in him when he first set out.

His little society in the colony has for the colonial the charm of a home in the provinces. It is chiefly made up of provincial elements from the home country. There may be a certain section from Algeria, the Antilles and Reunion—less than 15 per cent of the total; but the proportion of Europeans born in the colony is very small, scarcely 2 per cent; and that of retired persons minute—1 per cent, for the colonial may die in the colony, but he does not retire there. Such a society reflects France and its provinces in a very special way. It is a miniature, synthetic France, which includes North Africa and the Islands, and gathers together all the regions of France (with Corsica well to the fore) to make them sing in chorus in the provincial life of tropical Africa. The province has its own hierarchy which takes no account of the social classes from which its members have been recruited. One may picture this little European centre in native Africa: the postmaster speaks with the accent of Alsace, the schoolmaster with that of Marseilles; the doctor is not judged by his family or that of his wife. A small town, without families, but not without cliques.

It is a society in some respects migratory, with an incessant stream of internal mutations, besides the normal population changes (Ivory Coast in 1926: 3,200 Europeans—53 deaths, 26 marriages, 125 births).

20   FREEDOM AND AUTHORITY IN FRENCH WEST AFRICA

In arrivals and departures, the port of Dakar in 1937 handled 11,697 colonials, nearly half the total effectives of French West African Colonial Society. A strange migration without old people (on the Ivory Coast, only 11 Europeans are aged over 60), and where people are never exactly their own contemporaries, but sometimes, in the country of their childhood, behind, and sometimes, in the new world, ahead of the men they would have been had they stayed at home.

Are they intimately bound up with that home country? In thought and feeling, yes. Politically, no. The aeroplane brings to Dakar or Gao letters and Paris newspapers of the day before, yet events in Paris are followed with difficulty. They are not foreseen, and they hum as it were in a resonator which amplifies them inside the colonial brain. In May 1936, the colony was certain that the elections at home would not change the composition of Parliament. When the Popular Front victory was cabled, high-ranking officials thought that they would be recalled immediately—yet there was never the slightest question of recalling anyone. In normal times, the smallest item of news said to come from the Ministry or the head office of the firm at home assumes an unheard-of importance for the colonial official or the trading firm's agent. The very highest officials and the chief agents are not exempt from this. A Governor-General who has just left Paris, where he was sure he had the confidence of his Minister, is already worrying about whether he has lost it when he arrives in Dakar. Everything that happens at home is abnormal to the Colony. The most far-reaching reforms that have been brought to the colonies, such as the freeing of the slaves, were carried out under the pressure of home opinion, amid the stunned amazement or the criticism of Colonial Society—which does not imply that those reforms were always, I do not say right, but carried out in the right way.

The colonials feel the weakness of their minority position; they bear the weight of being Europeans, and they seek to concentrate their strength in a jealous exclusiveness. On leave or after retirement, instead of plunging into the main stream of society, they form a new colonial *milieu*. In a minority among the natives, they remain so among the metropolitans. If they are Europeans in the colony, they are colonials at home.

It is Bourgeois

Colonial Society bourgeois? At first glance, to stay-at-home French people, the thing seems impossible; as if colony meant the opposite of middle class; as if middle class meant thrift, moderation, decency. security, and colony meant extravagance, lawlessness, disordered living, danger. The black colonies seem to carry romance to absurd extremes. Mediterranean Africa can get away with it—it is exotic in a high-toned way. But the black colony seems to be associated with the idea of sin itself. The blacks are like damned souls in the shadow of evil, the heart of darkness. The colonial task must be left to the military and the missionaries, people who possess graces and immunities which a bourgeois could not lay claim to.

And yet the African colonies did not happen of their own accord, nor were they founded when our backs were turned, as has been said. In the nineteenth century the middle classes triumphed in France, and it was in the nineteenth century that France turned a large piece of Africa into colonies. Could this have been done without the strong bourgeoisie that held power? The French middle classes took to the mysterious continent with sentimental and matter of fact affection. What they loved in Africa was the possibility of applying their own civilization. They were conscious of the power given to them by the inventions of science. They were informed by the spirit of prophecy. The black colony seemed like the annexe to a universal exhibition adorned with allegorical figures of commerce and industry.

The bourgeois fact in Colonial Society is only properly understood when it is seen that the colony, far from being a lawless adventure, constitutes, above all, a concern of the State. The very nature of the native countries compelled the colony to be a State affair. There never were gentle savages in tropical Africa, virtuous children of nature living in blissful anarchy. The peoples we call primitive possessed a State which strictly regulated every detail of the relations between individuals and authority. There is nothing that favours individualism less than tribal life. The colony has only substituted one State for another. It could only impose itself on these countries by offering them another State in place of the old one. And in its colonial form, the State has the same aspect for the African territories as it had of old for the French provinces in Europe—it gathers the provinces together, centralizes administration and seeks unity.

Through the colony, the African countries were drawn towards the notion of the modern State. Moreover, although in France the State still allows some degree of economic liberalism, in the colony it has already decreed compulsory labour service, fixed commodity prices and wages and regulated production. In no colony of tropical Africa does the State confine itself to police functions; everywhere it

22 FREEDOM AND AUTHORITY IN FRENCH WEST AFRICA

tries its hand at fulfilling those of Providence. This is where things get complicated, and not the native areas only, but first of all Colonial Society, become closely subjected to the State. The Providence-State has more difficulties with the native areas than would a Police-State, and in order to solve them it invests Colonial Society with powers and lays on it tasks which deprive it of its liberty. It has to see to everything. The natives can no longer cut their lives into two, one part for themselves and the other for the colony. The colony has to shoulder everything—children in school as well as customary law in the courts. The colony becomes a sort of totalitarian party and the colonials compulsory members, working overtime to draw towards themselves the territory's whole native life. To act as Providence the colony has to find money, and to find money it has to call upon native labour under conditions which disturb the territory, and reinforce the influence of the State on Colonial Society.

Take the three great social objectives of French West Africa which obviously relate to the protection of humanity and the dignity of the individual: the freeing of the slaves, education and the fight against epidemics. To replace serf labour by a free peasantry, which means introducing machines and draught animals into the agrarian economy, and to recruit European teachers and doctors and train native ones, money must be raised by loans and taxes. Where is the money to be found? From major export products. But there can be no major export products without plantations and large-scale public works to blast an opening. Trade is indispensable to budgets. This forces the colony to construct harbours and roads, and to discover marketable produce and profitable agricultural methods. It is constrained to direct the natives to wage labour if not to compulsory labour. And thus they become a proletariat. The colony has proletarianized them in order to free them, educate them, care for them. In order to carry out social tasks, the colony has had to produce revenue, and to achieve this it has had to become commercial and thus has endowed its colonials with bourgeois characteristics; they enter the ranks of administration or commerce; they become officials or merchants.

Joseph Aynard in his essay 'La Bourgeoisie Française'[1] distinguishes two kinds of middle class: the commercial and the official. The commercial bourgeoisie of our maritime provinces turned very early to the African coast. Verdier, a shipbuilder and business man of La Rochelle, established a concession on the Ivory Coast which was to be one of the germs of the colony. An agent of his, Treich-Laplène,

[1] Bibliothèque du Musée Social, 1934.

COLONIAL SOCIETY

encountered Binger, on his way through the great forest. Merchants of Bordeaux and Ariège were foremost in the economic development of Senegal. In Africa itself, the reactions experienced were characteristically bourgeois. When proposals were made to liberate the right bank of the Senegal river from the oppressive rule of the Moorish overlords, there was stubborn opposition to expeditions into Mauritania. They had made Saint Louis a centre of bourgeois life, and that sufficed them; they distrusted military adventures. They preferred commerce to conquest, and the office—which they called 'the House' —to the imperialistic acquisition of territory.

Alongside the bourgeois merchant, you have his brother the official; next to the shop, the office. The official carries into the Tropics his cult of the centralized State. He administers with due respect for documents. He plays his historic part of the enemy of the feudal lords. He uproots them and strikes them down, not because they are black-skinned, but because they are like the barons and earls he knew in Europe. He brings to the service of the State an anti-feudal passion which he does not hesitate to direct against the commandants of the *cercles,* who love the fief they have found again, and for whom life does not consist of officialdom. He is suspicious of Governors who would like to act as enlightened despots. He is fanatically attached to the regulations—he personifies them.

Thus officials and merchants, bureaucrats and shopkeepers, serve the State and make money, in African countries where the native nobility did not conceive of the State in the same way as they did, and where the peasantry did not mix money matters with the cultivation of the soil. There are exceptions: the soldier and the priest, in so far as the former is not a bureaucrat with gold lace on nor the latter chaplain to the shops and offices. There would also be the planter, the settler, if he really owned as a patrimony the soil he cultivated, if he passed it on to his children like a family estate. But the proportion of such settlers in black Africa is negligible.[1] Indeed, since the two great motive forces in the colony are the State and money, and the former encroaches on the latter, it follows that colonial society is divided

---

[1] In the Ivory Coast where most of the planters are to be found, there were in 1938, 198 planters and 41 forest cultivators in a population of 3,200 Europeans. In Guinea there were 260 out of 1,697 Europeans. Guinea is very instructive:

Officials	341, of which 161 were at headquarters.
Army	139
Commerce	851 (304 at headquarters).
Agriculture	260 (all in three districts, Kindia, Dubuka and headquarters)
Missionaries	62
Others	44

24   FREEDOM AND AUTHORITY IN FRENCH WEST AFRICA

between Administration and Commerce, and that, sociologically speaking, it is bourgeois.

Finally, French colonial administrators are recruited from families already serving the State and Commerce. In the administration classes of the École National de la France d'outre-mer, of 259 pupils from 1930 to 1935 10·8 per cent only came from families of agricultural property owners; 35·5 per cent came from commerce and industry, and 53·7 per cent from the Army, administration in general and the professional middle class.

Objections will be made, on the score of the rough life and singular bearing of this bourgeoisie, and their impetuous conquest of Africa. It is true that this side of the work shines with a real brilliance, and deserves admiration. But why conceal the obverse, bourgeois side of the medal? It is excellently well struck. Go to those small colonial centres, and you will recognize them as provincial middle-class towns. They have their respectability and their Bohemianism. We cross the the swamp in a canoe, but it is to return a visit. We brush past yellow fever to take part in the social activities of a provincial town. We thrust aside lepers to enter a punctilious hierarchy and a formalism of endless documents. We pine for our families, our wives and children left in France, but even in the tropical heat we smile and bow in obedience to bourgeois conventions more compelling than any traditional fetish-worship. The commissions which His Britannic Majesty delivers in sterling to his District Officers of the Gold Coast, Sierra Leone and Nigeria, and the ranks bestowed by the French Republic upon its administrative officers in French West Africa, French Equatorial Africa and the Cameroons, constitute in fact a scale of bourgeois values. When the student of the École National de la France d'outre mer arrives at his African post, his first letter home is often a wail of disappointment: 'Is it for this that I have travelled so far?'—No, it is not for this, but the colony is what it is; it is often like that, and it is as well to know it.

What is serious is not that the colony, because it is in essence bourgeois, discourages adventure; but that the bourgeois frame of mind is no help to the colonial in getting to know the African territories. The disharmony is not, as people think, between the colonial frame of mind and the bourgeois, but between colonial society's bourgeois frame of mind and the native mind of the old Africa.

In Africa there is no black bourgeoisie outside the colony. But as a result of having been too frequently simply an extension of the European middle class, the colony has failed to understand the

COLONIAL SOCIETY

African chiefs, the patterns and the forces of native labour and ownership, the social structure of the country. Consequently it has not known how to reorganize the masses to whom it has brought disintegration. This will be shown in later chapters.

The glamour of colonial society has often been dimmed, not so much by the fact that it serves a bourgeois state bound up with money, but because it has often itself lacked money. This is the fault of the people at home, a fault which is clearly revealed in the history of the French African colonies in the nineteenth century. These colonies were like natural daughters whom one is reluctant to legitimize with the gift of a dowry. Out of a total budget estimated, before the 1914–18 war, at 113 thousand million francs, and which the bourgeoisie controlled because it controlled the banks, France allocated 40 thousand millions for foreign investments. How much did she lend to French West Africa? About 200 millions. The port of Dakar was passed over in favour of the port of Bahia. As a result of parsimony at home, fifteen million black people in French West Africa were abandoned. This fact still weighs on them, their colony is a daughter without a dowry. The huge French middle class, swollen by the addition of minor officials entrenched in their positions and workers who had made money, spent a century putting money by. It 'put by' for foreign countries and not for the colonies.

In the interests of the Government and of money the colony concentrates its shops and offices in the towns, and does not penetrate into rural areas; it does not embrace the country, but superimposes itself on it. It does not scatter its 25,000 or 28,000 Europeans among the fifteen million natives, one to every 600. It gathers them in clusters; 20,300 in thirty-two urban centres.[1] One of these centres

[1] Development of the European population in the towns.

	1934	1918
Dakar	10,250	2,791
Kaolack	620	200
Thiès	810	218
Saint-Louis	990	307

Concentration of Europeans in the towns:

In Senegal	14,500 in 14 centres
In the Soudan	1,400 ,, 5 ,,
In Guinea	1,750 ,, 4 ,,
On the Ivory Coast	1,850 ,, 5 ,,
In Dahomey	530 ,, 2 ,,
On the Niger	240 ,, 2 ,,
	20,270 32

Each one of these 32 centres counts at least 100 Europeans.

26 FREEDOM AND AUTHORITY IN FRENCH WEST AFRICA

alone, Dakar, contains almost half the Europeans of French West Africa. When the European population increases, don't think this means a new station set up in the bush; there is simply one more office or shop in the town. Colony headquarters are urban centres, often artificially constructed, and having something privileged and superfluous about them in relation to the country. There is an enormous difference between the African village and the colonial town, and even in the town between the native quarter and the European quarter. In the Soudan, where European houses were originally built of the local sun-dried brick (adobe), the contrast is not so marked, but it exists nevertheless. Europe and Africa take the same architectural nucleus, the same cubic cell; the former erects geometrical mansions, pierced at regular intervals by windows and doors, encircled with verandas, while the latter scatters a litter of miserable huts, when it does not camp out in petrol-tins, packing-cases, corrugated iron and scrap metal, the left-overs of the bourgeois colonial.

It is a Heroic Way of Organizing the World

Colonial Society, bourgeois though it is, has one characteristic which is the very opposite of bourgeois. A small number of business men and officials rise above Europe itself, in a more rigorous discipline than the service of the State or money. A personnel of high quality is devoted to organizing the world in a heroic way. The sentiment of heroic superiority which inspires colonial action is not racial or national. A black man, coming from the Antilles to the Congo or the Soudan as a colonial, shows himself as convinced of his superiority as if he were a dolichocephalic blond. The French wife of an English agent of the chartered Niger Company radiates authority as if she were a daughter of the stateliest home of England. The explanation is not only that the colonial is a European, but that he is something more. Far from Europe, he stands back at the right distance to measure its achievements. He realizes the permanent qualities, the essential values, the profound acquisitions of Europe, and learns that the ploughshare and the ox-yoke weigh heavier in the European balance than the scrap-iron of our machine age. He is conscious of acting on behalf of a certain eternal universalism. What he is creating and organizing in Africa goes far beyond Europe and its inhabitants, and to him the peoples living between the Mediterranean and the Baltic are simply other natives, those of the countries called metropolitan.

COLONIAL SOCIETY 27

His superiority derives not so much from his race or nation, as from the job he does and the moral and physical conditions in which he does it. The harder these conditions are, the more heroically he struggles. The colonial knows more about many things than the natives of colonial territories, and has a truer appreciation of their value than those other natives—the colonizing powers. He really pays the price of civilization, and not in money but in trouble and danger. Nowadays he has a refrigerator, a car, a wireless set, and yet the colony is still not an easy place. The European in Europe lives like a parasite, taking material progress for granted; in Africa he earns it by his own efforts. This makes him a trifle off-hand with the tourist from home visiting the colonies, who thinks that in taking his ticket for the trip he has bought a right both to Africa and to comfort. The colonial pays for his seat—and his ice—by staying put in the heat.

The better the colonial understands the power of civilized man, the more he knows it to be mingled with death. He can count on his fingers his own expectation of life: ten tours of two years each, which makes twenty sea trips, and his account is put paid to, ready for the records office. He ages quickly—the records of deaths among retired officials show a figure seventeen years below the average.

The people of the home countries, even when they beat the tom-tom of imperialism, do not understand what the small white company of colonials endures, how stiff is the test of body and soul. The up-rooting of every departure, the home that is only kept together by letters, the absence of children who are growing up so far away, unsettled health, the constant effort needed to master one's work in a new country every tour and in a society which has its moods and fevers; the rains and the travelling—everything conspires to give life in the colonies a broken rhythm, a tormented and fitful character. It would be easy to etch an acid picture of colonial society as a collection of sick men: the obese, carrying before them toad-like bellies, contrasted with the living skeletons, fleshless from fever or drained by dysentery; the liver cases, their eyes by turns dulled or too bright, bowed by that inner gnawing; the nervous types, who, the moment they are back from leave, wilt under the burden of overwork and see no way to lighten it. As late as 1929, the Governor-General of French West Africa solemnly read out in Government Council the number of Europeans' days in hospital: in that year, among 16,000 Europeans, 5,241 hospital cases, 83,291 hospital days. Amid this dolorous company, starved of natural air and health, what moral misery, what bile stewing in the sun, but also what silent self-sacrifice! This liverish

28 FREEDOM AND AUTHORITY IN FRENCH WEST AFRICA

accountant, doubled up over his cash-box full of tax-money, was supporting a dependent niece in France out of his pay. This trader dropped his business to accompany at his own expense the wife of an airman trying to find her husband, thought to have come down in the forest. Colonials, they say, are apostles or beasts. No, the best and the worst of them are equally soldiers in the same battle, and not one of them is without his wounds.

You need to have a vocation for this life of sacrifice. The famed liberty of colonial life lies in this vocation. I always ask the high-school pupils who pass top of the lists in the entrance examination to the École National: 'Why did you want to come here?' All the answers throb with the desire for freedom. Will they be free, these colonial residents, these boarders in Africa? Yes, if they really have the vocation, they will breathe liberty in every corner of Africa where they may serve. Their comrade Bernard stood for liberty among the Somalis at Dikkil where he was killed in 1935. An ex-teacher, now Governor of Djibouti, has just sent the students photos of the station —a few bare huts in the dry bush with a low surrounding wall which Bernard called the 'tronillomètre'. Now, in front of the wall, is the tomb of this twenty-five-year-old assistant administrator, but the pulsating liberty of which the students of the school dream can still be felt. And this feeling haunts everyone who, having known it in the colony, in the Administration, on the plantations or in commerce, has been deprived of it on returning to France. Cabined and confined in his retirement, the official indulges in regrets, but the commercial agent or the planter tries to get back into the game at any cost.

The colony is not composed entirely of illustrious leaders, heroes in Carlyle's sense of the word, who change the face of the world. The heroic quality clothes the clerk as well as the Governor-General, the small trader worming his way in the native markets as well as the captain of industry launching a deal.

When the colonial lives in the isolation of the bush, the heightening of his personality is all the more striking because it generally takes place in the neighbourhood of communities where loss of individuality seems to be the rule. Against the background of these African peoples the colonial stands out with a personality all the stronger because he seems to be alone in having one. But it sometimes happens that he modifies it or strips himself of it to the point of losing it altogether. And there you have a fresh quality of Colonial Society.

COLONIAL SOCIETY 29

Colonial Society is acted upon by the Native Territory

The native territories crowd in upon Colonial Society from every side and act upon it. It is one of the major themes of colonial literature, this secret empire exercised over a man by a country of which he counts himself the master. But even when he goes to the colonies not as a dilettante but as a builder, not vanquished by life but to conquer a new life, the colonial is acted upon by the native country.

One of the more notable proofs of this contention is the fact that colonials of different nationality serving in similar native territories resemble one another more closely in certain respects than do colonials of the same origin serving in different native countries. A factory manager in the Belgian Congo and a trader of French Senegal, the Commandant of a *cercle* in the Niger province and a District Officer in Nigeria, have more in common as regards their professions than the Commandant of the Niger and the Resident in Cambodia. So great is the influence of the territory administered that it overrules the nationality of the administrators; so insidious the power of the land prospected that it penetrates into the prospectors. A Frenchman of Africa and an Englishman of Africa have characteristics in common, African characteristics, marking them as clearly as the national bond that links a Frenchman of Africa to a Frenchman of Asia, and all the more remarkable in that French colonials and English colonials do not mix together much.

Another proof is the feudal spirit: it is as if the white chiefs had taken the colour of the native chiefs. And every white man is tempted to make himself a feudal ruler, especially when he lacks general culture.

The question of concubinage, mixed marriages and mulattoes.

It is impossible to discuss the action of the native country on Colonial Society without referring to the question of concubinage, of mixed marriages and miscegenation.[1] 'It is a question of individuals or of circumstances, rather than a question of race or class,' wrote Delafosse in 1923 in a study made for the International Colonial Institute. But the position of the mulatto is not an individual but a social question. The half-breed son usually enters the father's environment, the daughter that of the mother. Miscegenation by

[1] On the Ivory Coast, the 1936 census gave 3,200 Europeans, 3,846,000 natives, 600 mulattoes.

30   FREEDOM AND AUTHORITY IN FRENCH WEST AFRICA

white women being very rare in the colonies (less so in the metro-polises), half-breed boys are thus brought up as Europeans, and the girls as natives (if they are not casually abandoned to orphanages). In reality the situation of half-breeds depends on whether or not their legal position corresponds to their social status. In the French colonies the half-breed, either legitimate or legitimized, is in law a European, but socially, owing to colour prejudice, this is not so.

The education and fate of the half-breed child are not the same within marriage as outside it. Governments have been known to encourage mixed marriages, and nowadays do not forbid them. In British colonies, where the colour bar reigns, it would seem that the problem of the half-breed does not exist; but actually it is there. And it is all very well for South Africa to treat intercourse between a black woman and a white man as a delict in her case but not in his—the number of half-breeds there is increasing. In the French colonies of black Africa, mixed marriages were frequent in the early days; Saint-Louis-in-Senegal and Gorée were the home of the *seignares*; the word is a corruption of *seigneur*—the half-breed was a gentleman. The number of mulattoes is declining in number since the advent of the white woman.

Mulattoes have played a considerable part in the history of the colony. They have gone into commerce, administration and the Councils. They may even become so well integrated into the colony that they arouse native hostility. Their function is not yet at an end. They are still the only people, among blacks and whites, who can tap the hidden sources of an existence where Africa and Europe blend so intimately.

The Africanization of the Colony.

The country acts on the colony even more strongly by Africanizing it outright. The so-called *évolués* are effecting an entrance into the ranks of the administrative and commercial staffs of the colony. In the Education Department, for example, there are 200 European and 650 native teachers.

This Africanization has been accelerated by a number of causes: politically, the natives have acquired rights, and in particular that of collaborating in administration; financially, their collaboration costs less than that of Europeans. This sharing of public functions by Euro-peans and natives is a notable revolution; since the colony exercises a sort of trusteeship over the native territory, natives are taking an increasing part in it. Nearly always, it was the conquering army

COLONIAL SOCIETY 31

which first set the example, by recruiting natives forthwith as regular soldiers and subaltern officers.[1] Africanization in second-grade administrative posts has become the rule. (In the intermediate and higher posts it is blocked by the obligation laid on the official to possess the status of French citizen.) It is a known fact that the majority of the electors of Senegal are black, and that they have wrested the seat of Deputy from the whites and mulattoes ever since the election of 1913.

In commerce, Africanization is proceeding actively. In native Africa, on the Gold Coast and in Nigeria, on the Ivory Coast and in Dahomey and Senegal, a merchant middle class is being born which uses cars and bank accounts, and is becoming economically powerful,[2] putting its sons into the liberal professions and ruining the political power and prestige of the traditional chiefs.

These are the *évolués*. What does this term mean? They are 'evolved' rather than 'evolving'. They are perhaps those who are now developing the least. They have managed to penetrate into the State and Commerce in the colony. They observe its laws and defend its privileges. They have Africanized an organism that has absorbed them. They have dyed it their colour, but they have not transformed it by their spirit. They are sometimes as far removed from the native masses as a white man could be, or farther. They too are town-dwellers,[3] office and shop staffs, tenants of a superstructure. Nevertheless they are involved in a new and profound social movement.

THE COMMANDANT OF THE 'CERCLE' IN COLONIAL SOCIETY

Whatever his age, his rank, his race, the Commandant of the *Cercle* is chief in his territory. He is not the representative of Colonial Society, nor its delegate exercising its authority in the native territories. He represents public authority *vis-à-vis* the colonials as well as

---

[1] The African Army raised during the 1914–18 War numbered 175,000 men. In 1938 its effectives were distributed thus in French West Africa:
(a) Europeans: Officers and equivalent ranks, 510. N.C.O.s and O.R.s, 2,531. Total, 3,041.
(b) Natives: Officers and N.C.O.s, 2,369. O.R.s, 12,101. Total, 14,470.
(c) Special levy of *tirailleurs* in 1938, 12,000. Grand total, 29,511.
In France, North Africa and in other colonies there were 30,000 native troops over and above those in French West Africa.

[2] One native trader had the amount of his fortune engraved on his tombstone.

[3] Of 40,000 native inhabitants of the town of Kaolack, half have only been there for the last fifteen years. They are former country people, who have got rich and let out their fields of groundnuts to the Navetanes. The women wanted to move into town. They no longer pound millet; the family eats rice bought in shops with the money from the leased fields.

32 FREEDOM AND AUTHORITY IN FRENCH WEST AFRICA

the natives. He may be a young Deputy Administrator, third class, he may be black or white, but no official of another service, no trader, no planter, however important, may encroach upon his authority or try to make use of it for his own ends.

The Commandant knows that a colony, by definition, must possess a responsible metropolitan country. He embodies the responsibility of France in the corner of Africa where he is chief. He knows that there can be no colony without the guardianship of the mother country, or without a native territory which collaborates within that guardianship in the creation of a new world. He personifies that collaboration. Only by means of co-ordinated action can he be the leader.

He must beware of the small-town life: it will hinder him from acting by tempting him to ostentation or intrigue; or else it will overwhelm him with details to the point of encroaching on his official duties. It will require him to supply it with vegetables, fruit, chickens, cajoling him by flattery: You are the only one, Commandant, who can get anything done!

In Colonial Society he acts as chief by understanding the Europeans of the different services and callings, and co-ordinating their activities, for the benefit of native life, for the building of a new world. He visits, receives, consults the teacher, the doctor, the head of the postal services, the engineer, the trader, the planter, the officer, the missionary. He knows that people in Colonial Society are strongly marked by their calling, and that each profession has its forceful social type. He understands that a carrier, who breaks his back at the wheel of a lorry, in the sun by day, by the light of his headlamps at night, has not the same weakness for the bush as a Treasury clerk, to whom the offer of a jaunt in a car means a joyful release. He has sufficient general culture to respect the independence of real specialists and to leave their work to them. Nothing is more ludicrous than an administrator who airs decided views on everything, on public works to the engineer, on medicine to the doctor.

He does not forget that he is responsible to his Governor, and that the Governor is surrounded by departments with which he must keep on good terms. He must enjoy the confidence of his Governor and day by day he must sink himself deeper into his own job. He is required, by regulation, to keep a diary, and this gives him an opportunity to weigh up the relative importance of the colony and the native territories, and to judge whether, in his administration, he gives to each its due. Has a day gone by in which nothing of impor-

COLONIAL SOCIETY

tance to the natives has come to his notice? Then he may fear that he has been too much concerned with the colonial community. Let him keep one day in the week free from the colonials and entirely devoted to the natives, not counting the days spent on tour in the bush.

The minority character of Colonial Society is constantly in his mind, not only in the small stations where there is only one white man, but just as much in a big district where the European nucleus is of considerable size, and where one is tempted to think that the native masses are merely its satellites. In the *Cercle* of Bobo-Diou-lasso, for example, it is true there are 242 Europeans, but there are also 295,000 natives; at Ouagadougou, 160 Europeans but also 469,000 natives. But here, as elsewhere, the Commandant is Chief for all of them, and must not sacrifice either to the other; moreover, he would be wrong to think that an increase in the number of whites automatically enhances his authority over the native mass. He is mistaken if he imagines that he will rule the country better because he appears to belong to a colonial society which is slightly less of a minority.

Whatever the proportion—or disproportion—of the number of Europeans to natives, the Commandant always has to try to harmon-ize the colony and the native territory. And whatever the numbers, he is only the chief so long as he remains the sole chief. If he has colleagues he can indeed share the work, but not his responsibility.

French tropical Africa, though it may multiply its colonials ten or a hundred times, will not endure except by the same means which brought it into existence. It was created by individual officers, who formed a team indeed, but only because they were all animated by the same spirit of personal devotion to their work in the native terri-tories, where they functioned as individuals. Whatever they did—founding a station, making a road, compiling a grammar—they worked at a deep level. They did not talk about their authority; it was within them and grew from their way of living. They radiated a natural authority because they worked in the isolation of a ruler.

This rule does not change. It is oneself, not one's neighbour, that must be mastered; it is the cultivation of one's own soul that one must labour at. The Commandant does not attain to his position except through the strength of his interior life. In him, in his own person, resides the ineffaceable dignity and the indivisible responsi-bility of the chief. And it is in solitude that his interior life grows and develops so that he does not exact obedience because of his rank, but acts with authority because of his character.

III. THE NATIVE TERRITORIES

THE INDIGENOUS POPULATIONS

IN relation to the colony, the native territories are the masses: fifteen million natives in the Federation of French West Africa, which includes the colonies of Mauritania, Senegal, Soudan, Guinea, Ivory Coast, Dahomey and Niger; five million in the British colonies of the Gambia, Gold Coast and Sierra Leone; twenty million in British Nigeria on the eastern flank of A.O.F. From Cap Blanc to the Gulf of Benin, from Senegal to the Benue, stretches this mass of forty million Africans, with zones of density varying from three per square kilometre for the whole of French West Africa to twenty for Nigeria and twenty-four for Sierra Leone. Within the mass there is a seasonal flow of migratory currents, generally from the interior to the coast.

Up to the nineteenth century, the Europeans planted their African colonies in settlements along the fringe of the continent and not in the continent itself. On this strip arose the trading posts, the forts, the wharves for overseas shipping. The colonial activity of the nineteenth century consisted in widening these strips, linking them to each other, making trade gravitate towards them and political influence spring up around them, and in starting to penetrate into the interior. Thus the colony moved towards the country, like some force the movement of which was to be speeded up more and more by a new coefficient, the coefficient of the native mass. Indeed, the conquest of Africa was a series of political operations rather than a large-scale military expedition. The natives, far from being exterminated or driven out by the conquest, were made use of as soldiers and then installed as producers.

At the time of the settlements, the natives had no demographic and economic weight. It was towards the end of the nineteenth century that their increase began to make itself felt. In 1830, France had less than 15,000 Africans in her West African settlements—a century later she had fifteen million of them to govern. Tribal wars had ceased; the slave trade, which had drained the countries' substance for 250 years,

THE NATIVE TERRITORIES 35

had been stopped; slavery had been extirpated. The population acquired a new strength that modified the conditions of colonial rule as it did those of native rule. It was no longer a question of transporting slaves, nor of domesticating them on the spot, but of directing a social force.

The mass still seems passive, but it has acquired the power inherent in production; French West Africa produces 500,000 tons of groundnuts and 50,000 tons of cocoa for the world market; the value of its exports amounted to 864,792,000 francs in the first six months of 1938. It consumes during the year more than a billion francs' worth of imported goods. The purchasing power of this mass has become of engrossing concern to the workers of Europe, who are unemployed if its production fails.

Across all administrative frontiers, the mass to-day exhibits the same feelings and reactions, and everywhere it sets the same essential problem: its relationships with its chiefs, native as well as European.

The words of Henri de Man, referring to the masses in Europe, may also be applied to Africa. 'The bureaucrat is not a real leader; he dominates or acts as an instrument of domination. . . . Only those can be leaders who are not afraid of the masses whom they have to lead. . . . The choice of a leader means the choice of the bravest man.' The leader will be 'a brave fighter and a cultured man, whose social conscience has been sharpened by knowledge, but also a man who has no fear of any worldly power which might prevent him from putting into practice what his social conscience dictates'.[1]

UNDERSTANDING THE AFRICAN TERRITORIES

No colonial administrator can flatter himself that he knows everything that history, geography, ethnology, linguistics and sociology can teach him about the African territories. He will only have time to get the merest sketch of the scene in which he will have to act. Here is the attitude of mind he must maintain if he is to see things straight:

He must distinguish clearly between the colony and the native territory. There is no question of dissociating these two elements; on the contrary, the art of administration consists in binding them firmly together. But in order fully to understand them it is necessary to study them separately. The administrator, more than any other colonial, must be aware of the native territory.

[1] Henri de Man, *Masses et Chefs*, Brussels, 1931 (quoted by E. Lefranc in *Tribune des fonctionnaires*, 23 April 1938).

36 FREEDOM AND AUTHORITY IN FRENCH WEST AFRICA

He must realize, in the first place, that the colony is scarcely ever confronted with one country only. As a rule the colony is based on an artificial grouping of regions, like the different geographical regions within a Department in France. Furthermore, the earliest colonists, who concentrated their efforts on uniting territories and subduing native chiefs, seldom understood the structure of those territories. Thus the colony presents the appearance of an aggregation of territories, which were dominated politically and transformed economically before the societies of which they were formed had been explored.

In the territories, there are certain forms of social life which are difficult for colonials to understand, because they no longer have any equivalent in the historical consciousness of the home country: nomadism, for instance. The African nomads, Moors (450,000 souls), Targui (270,000), Fulani (1,965,000), are far less amenable to colonial conditions than the sedentary cultivators. These nomads happen to be of Semitic race: they are whites. It is thus not too paradoxical to assert that in negro Africa the white natives are the most 'savage' of all.

There is one great difference between the colony and the native territories: negro Africa knew nothing of urban life. The Dutch writer, de Kat Angelino, in his book, *The Colonial Problem*, makes the same statement with regard to Asia, and affirms that the attraction which native life has for colonials is a form of nostalgia for a far-distant past, for a primitive Europe before the cities of the Greeks and Romans, the towns of the Renaissance and the Hanseatic league, or the Communes of Flanders, had glorified the long reign of urban life. There are in Africa vast native agglomerations, like a number of villages placed side by side, but there is no such thing as a truly African urban spirit. Timbuctoo owes its urban character to the Moroccans, Porto-Novo to the Portuguese.

Another difference lies in the character of labour. This is relatively recent—the early explorers were not conscious of it. They were able to understand the rural and artisan labour of Africa. If distance, climate, manners made them feel strange, African labour made them feel at home again. The crops were different, but the spirit and the tools were the same as in the Europe of that time. Millet instead of wheat, but the same sickle; cotton instead of flax, but the same actions in spinning and weaving.

When the explorers were replaced by colonizers everything was changed. Founding a colony is not simply adding to the mother country an economy which, though its natural features are alien, is fundamentally the same kind of society; it is rather developing the African territories by means of a new economic organization. Strangely enough, the colonial in Africa has never been intolerant towards native religions, but he has been intolerant of native labour, with a lack of understanding amounting to oppression, and which is only now beginning to be abandoned. In his plans for large-scale enterprises and production, he lost sight of the workers and producers, and made no study of the methods of labour and production indigenous to the country.

Thus, while on the moral and political level he thought of the blacks as men, on the economic plane he treated them as man-power. We shall see how this mistake has for a long time kept out of sight the existence of an agragrian problem and the future of the African peasantry.

The administrator should not think that the native territories lead a narrow social existence. The richness of their social life has never disappointed those who have studied it. And it should be studied without prejudice.

The Government of French West Africa causes its administrators to proceed from the Stone Age to the age of petrol. There is a risk here that the different territories may be graded in a hierarchy, and those of the petrol age be ranked above those of the Stone Age. It is convenient to say that one country is advanced and another backward, but this manner of speaking spoils one's judgment. Special attention will be given to the territory regarded as advanced, while the so-called backward one will be neglected; or else the backward country will be credited with an imaginary innocence, because of its backwardness, and attempts will be made to preserve this fictitious quality. The noble fellows of the bush will be praised at the expense of the degenerates at headquarters.

There are few prejudices as hardy as this and as harmful to healthy administration. In reality, no country is a bad one to the good administrator.

Moreover, it is not only the *évolués* who are advancing. The masses are far from static. The 2,340,000 passengers on the French West African railway system in 1935 were not all educated. The population, whether splintered into an infinity of tribes, or gathered together into nations, has broken its traditional structure under the pressure of colonial forces; in so doing it has assumed mass importance, but not in order to remain motionless. Levelling and rais-

38   FREEDOM AND AUTHORITY IN FRENCH WEST AFRICA

ing, stamping and pummelling the earth on public and private construction jobs in the urban centres; working off labour service far from the village; looking for work, as an agricultural labourer on groundnut, banana, cocoa, coffee, cotton and sisal plantations, sometimes a thousand miles from home; as a soldier further still, in Morocco, France, Syria—the tribesman has become a man of the masses in the midst of an Africa even newer than we thought it. And how could he himself not be a new man too? He comes and goes on the roads in a ceaseless journey, a petty trader here, a labourer there, and always cut off from his family. The mass that he enters into moves in a way that we are only imperfectly aware of, and it is sometimes carried right off the paths we thought it had taken and along which we wished to lead it. It does not keep to the rules that have guided the evolution of the natives within the colony. A trivial, but significant instance: while the literates get their clothes European fashion through the mail-order catalogues of the big Paris department stores, the mass will reject the bush storekeeper's striped cotton cloth which took its fancy the year before; to the great surprise of the storekeeper and of the buyers at head office it will demand cloth all of one pastel colour and stiffly finished.

There is a dim apprehension that the mass is being moved by feelings which it cannot make intelligible and which may impel it to inexplicable migrations or to an inertia which will be put down to laziness.

In the former colony of the Upper Volta the political situation presented no problems. There were no educated natives, or so few! And the Mossi people seemed well under the control of their natural chiefs, the *nabas*. One day, the London *Times* learned from its Paris correspondent that a Mossi migration had taken place from the Upper Volta to the Gold Coast and that it had provided the native cocoa-producers of that colony with nearly 100,000 plantation workers. It was some time before the cause of this mass movement was recognized: the Upper Volta colony had ordered the native chiefs—the *nabas*—to have cotton grown on a large scale. The *nabas* had tried to make each village cultivate a collective cotton-field, invoking ancient local customs: a feudal one of the manorial domain, where the village works for its lord; and a communal one of the common field, where the village works for itself. In fact, the feudal custom was only observed in the case of traditional crops, and the communal custom only worked when the people decided on it themselves. Befogged by the need to work fast, the colony thought it could

THE NATIVE TERRITORIES 39

build its new economy on the ancient social order; claiming to act in virtue of native custom, it rendered the custom burdensome—and inoperative. To free themselves from this forced cultivation, the natives quickly and quietly emigrated to the neighbouring foreign colony, the Gold Coast. The territorial administrators got no hearing from the people in Government offices, whose heads were turned by the cotton experts. And one of the best organized and hierarchical peoples of negro Africa displayed a reaction and took a direction that it would have been wise to study—instead of denying its existence.[1]

THE COLONIAL ADMINISTRATION AND THE NATIVE TERRITORIES

There is no lack of documentation, some of it now produced by Africans themselves. At the 1931 Colonial Exhibition the *Congrès de la Société Indigène*, organized by Georges Hardy, showed the work done by native investigators who were discovering their own country by methods we have taught them. They hold in their black or copper-coloured hands the future development of such knowledge.

The Bulletin of the Education Department of French West Africa, inspired by Albert Charton, has assembled a team of instructors—African and European—who together study the children, the environment, the means of livelihood, the life of a district. Administrators, officials, doctors, civil servants of all kinds and ranks, and missionaries all read Levy-Bruhl and carry on the work of research. It is no longer unknown lands, but African life which is being explored. The work of Delafosse is being carried on by Lt. Desplagues, by Capt. Urvoy, by the Administrator Tauxier, by Labouret, by Dr. Cremer, by Waterloot the master printer. Robert Randau, René

---

[1] In *L'Afrique Française* of February 1939, in an article entitled 'Côte d'Ivoire 1939', Labouret estimates the number of workers who emigrated annually from the Upper Volta to the Gold Coast, at 100,000 and notes that most of them refused to take up employment in public or private enterprises in the Ivory Coast. He adds that when he wanted to study this problem in the course of a mission to the Gold Coast, in 1929, he was unable to arouse the slightest interest in his enterprise at Dakar.

Between 1912 and 1938 the population of the Gold Coast has doubled, from 1,700,000 to 4,000,000 inhabitants. British observers consider that this is due, among other causes, to a steady stream of French natives emigrating from the Upper Volta. They give four reasons for this migration:

(1) Irregular military recruiting in 1918 (to which Vollenhoven was opposed).
(2) Abuse of forced labour.
(3) Compulsory cotton growing.
(4) Bad monetary organization and lack of those provincial budgets in which the native can see for himself the use to which his money is put.

There is yet another reason. On the Gold Coast the Volta Africans work for other Africans and in the native way. On the Ivory Coast they have to work for Europeans and in the European way.

40 FREEDOM AND AUTHORITY IN FRENCH WEST AFRICA

Mardu, André Demaison are writing their stories of African life. A young administrative officer, Gilbert Vieillard and a retired colonel and Governor, Gaden, are studying the Fulani. Members of the civil service who take a course at the Ecole Coloniale bring with them material for an ethnological thesis on the district where they have served. Paul Rivet founded the Musée de l'Homme and sent Griaule to Bandiagara. Besides the *Bulletin* of the Comité de l'Afrique Française, where Auguste Terrier has been succeeded by Ladreit de Lacharriere, and the *Bulletin* of the Comité d' Études de l'Afrique Occidentale Française, which owes so much to Henry Hubert, numerous other publications are available to students: the *Bulletin* of the Service d'Information de L'A.O.F. at Dakar, and of the Service Intercolonial d'Information in Paris, *Africa, Outre-Mer*, the *Monde Colonial Illustré*, the journal of the Société des Africanistes, the Negro section at the Centre d'Études de Politique Étrangère—so many centres of information and study. No colour bar divides those engaged on this great task. In the commission of enquiry appointed in 1936 and dissolved in July 1938 for lack of funds, Henri Labouret made a point of including scientifically trained native investigators— Paul Hazoumé,[1] Manby Sidibe and Amadon Mapaté Diagne.

Now, after half a century of colonization, following on half a century of exploration, there are so many Europeans who have studied Africa systematically that the colonial—who has merely lived there —feels at a disadvantage, and begins to doubt what he thought he knew. Nevertheless he knows that he should seek up-to-date information about the condition of women in Mossi from Sister Marie-André of the Sacred Heart; light on the cultures of the Sahara from Theodore Monod; a description of native drama from Bernard Maupoil. Moreover, his doubts are increased when he notices that the natives are beginning to study their own cultures. A point has been reached where the ordinary life of an administrator can no longer include all these studies. Exploration in depth has begun; wells are being sunk and tunnels bored beneath the country-side where officials live and move, and discoveries are being made which upset administrative routines.

The colonial administrator—the Commandant—cannot ignore these activities, and he can assist them, but for him it is essential to know the country by direct experience in relation to the needs of his

---

[1] Paul Hazoumé, a Government teacher in Dahomey, published a novel, *Doguicimi*, which was awarded a prize in 1939 by the adjudicators of the Prix Littéraire de l'Empire.

THE NATIVE TERRITORIES 41

job and the problems of his position. He must, then, approach the territory with sympathy and discernment. Unless he expects to find humanity—individual men—in the remotest tribe and the most impermeable mass, he will never make contact with that vital current which will put him into communication with that tribe and that mass. Nevertheless he will have to exercise a certain reserve, in order to preserve his clear-sightedness.

He will make it clear that he has faith in the country; he will draw the people to himself, but he will be on his guard against trickery, and will seek to discover the springs of action appropriate to the place and time. The Mossi country cannot be governed by the same methods as are used in Mauritania, nor are the methods of 1908 suitable to 1938.

Trust is not born simply from contact and distrust does not necessarily result from a clash. There is no better discipline in case of mistrust and no better means to mutual trust than to get a job done together, with the administrator himself taking part in it, physically as well as morally.

He should get away from his usual sedentary life. At his station, he only meets certain natives—they are always the same ones, and they belong to the colony rather than to the country. The wives of his guards get him to settle their domestic disputes. The interpreters keep him turning in a narrow circle of intrigues. He looks after his garden as if he were retired, he fiddles about with buildings and furnishings. From time to time he is aware of taxpayers, litigants, labour service workers—but not of free men in their own country. Because he has no office hours and can function in pyjamas, he thinks he is in the bush. In fact, he is a mere bureaucrat and not a leader in action.

If he cannot leave his station, let him at least take some antidote to this hermit's waltzing sickness. Let him make out a calendar of the country in almanack fashion, with the seasons of cultivation, the fairs and markets and holidays.

The best ways of learning all involve a personal effort, and there are at least two—the vernacular language, and going on tour.

The Language

Which native language should he choose? There are 400 in French West Africa, and several in every district. To select one is to run the risk of taking sides politically for one country against the others. Do the Serers of Senegal like a French administrator to harangue them in Wolof? Would the Comtois like to be addressed by the mayor in the

42   FREEDOM AND AUTHORITY IN FRENCH WEST AFRICA

dialect of Burgundy? The Senufos will not be afraid to reply through an interpreter to an administrator who questions them in French, but they will be silent if he uses Dioula, the language of their former oppressors. With these reservations it may be said that there are some vernacular languages which are widely used. It is an advantage everywhere to know Fulani, Mandingo and Hausa—and, on the coast of Guinea, Pidgin, which constitutes a colonial language— native French, with a vocabulary and syntax which are worth study. The administrator can often benefit from the advice of missionaries and of European traders and planters, whom the country has adopted, if only because they know the language and can amplify, correct or verify what the official interpreter says.

In general, collaboration with European residents will provide the administrator with sources of information. In the Gold Coast, District Officers learn much not only through their use of the Hausa language, which is obligatory, but also because of their contacts with members of the agricultural department who visit native plantations and hear the news in the course of discussions about cocoa and coffee.

The Art of going on Tour

When I consider the function of the head of a district and attempt to expound it in the light of my own experience, I find in the tour of the villages its essential principle and its peculiar charm.

If we did not go on tour, we should merely be a body of officials superimposed on the country; it is on tour that we learn to know it and keep it fast, by taking it in the right way, from the inside; and here also we taste at the same time the pleasures of travel and of being the chief.

Above all, there should be no rigid rule either in the method or the object of a tour. The motor car and the plane can be combined with travel on horseback or on foot; a census or a judicial enquiry with informal palavers or even with a tour having no special object —which is a delicate but effective art.

Governor Jacques Fousset used to say that sitting at the wheel of a car was much the same as sitting at a desk—it does not necessarily change one's outlook. But it is not a bad thing to use a car to get off the road which one has already seen and in a few hours reach the place where one gets into the native territory. And a tour by car, if it is done properly, throws light on the life of the roads on which the

THE NATIVE TERRITORIES   43

lorries ply; on the carriers' trips, the habits of native drivers and where they put up overnight, and on the stream of trade and news kept going by these transport monsters. The plane will show us at a stroke the features of a whole region, unknown villages with their hidden lands, and will allow us to record the state of cultivation and to follow its progress. In Senegal in 1932, Leon Geismar, inspector of agricultural production, was able to report, by means of aerial surveys, on the results achieved in the bush by cultivators of groundnuts and millet.

Thus plane and car have their uses, but they are limited ones; contact with the country is not established by flying over it any more than by dashing through it. When moving at a horse's pace, or at the rate of the porters, one enters more completely into one's district than when travelling at speed, and the villages as one approaches them at a natural rhythm are prepared for one's coming.

Heat and thirst used to torment us, sending us countless times to the tin can to drink the same mouthful of tepid water; but these things are only remembered in order to recall meetings and greetings with the travellers on the old roads of Africa—pedlars, hunters, musicians, pilgrims.

The new roads, like the ancient tracks, have their wisdom; they are like snakes which must be charmed if one would hear their secrets. But if the new inter-colonial roads, splashed with motor oil and striped with tyre tracks, unroll a new Africa, the paths trodden through sand, rock and grass know the oldest stories.

Our forebears passed that way: explorers and soldiers, Rene Caillié with his compass hidden under his Egyptian dress, Binger with two servants, eight donkeys and his own common sense. That is the way the colony was made, and thus it is maintained. The more the bush can see the Commandant in his uniform coming on horseback or on foot along the old paths, the more will the new African world across all the continent draw from a deep spring life for its arteries, for its miles of railways and roads, and its surface studded with harbours and airfields.

On my first real journey in native Africa, during the eleven stages from Kano to Zinder, I learnt once and for all a number of things about pack-camels and pack-oxen, and how the caravan-men must not be hurried, nor a start made against the guide's advice when a tornado threatens. I have never forgotten those eleven days. Intoxicated as I was with my new rank of Deputy Administrator and my pride at being posted up country, I was really being schooled by

44 FREEDOM AND AUTHORITY IN FRENCH WEST AFRICA

Africa in the Soudan class. My masters were nameless men, whose lesson I was to understand later. For instance, that human apparition who helped us to cross the swamp; he went ahead to show us the winding ford, and poured out from a calabash libations of the water which had to be magically entreated on our behalf. The file of camels, immersed to the neck, wet to the hump, seemed changed into yellow plucked swans, as they lifted invisible and clumsy pads stirring up the water which terrified them. I was perched on a sort of shield held up by four men, amphibian caryatides. Motionless and useless, I was nevertheless part of the caravan, and merely by watching attentively I shared the collective ordeal under the guidance of the spellbinder of the ford. Then there was an old man who had asked me on the morning we left for permission to go along with us. He followed us all those eleven days, his only luggage a mat, saying not a word except when he unrolled his mat at each stop to recite the Koranic prayer. As the years go by, his temperance and his piety grow more striking in memory, and I think, not without shame, of the case of aperitifs which I had brought with me, and of my arrogant illusions as a young colonial. In the course of my service, as tour followed tour, never without some adventure, the thought often occurred to me that my first steps into the bush were taken under the eyes of the two ancient religions of Africa: fetishism and Islam; and though I did not really understand them, at least I did not look on them with contempt. And afterwards, whenever, in the villages, I came across a mosque or a sacrificial altar of baked clay, I approached them without fear, as if we had already forged an acquantance far away from the habitations of men.

Not the least of the advantages of going on tour is that one approaches the villages through a world of sensations which those who work in an office cannot perceive; and a further advantage is that the conception of the native masses is restored to its right proportions in one's mind, when one has seen with one's own eyes the diversities of the country and the exact situation of each human habitation. The Commandant must be conscious of the mass existence of the natives, but he must also realize their distribution into local peasant populations; these present a social problem but in a very different form from that presented by industrial societies. He is confronted, on the one hand by 100, 200, 300 thousand natives, and on the other by these same people divided into their countries, embedded in their villages.

The Commandant can constantly correct his action on the mass by

THE NATIVE TERRITORIES   45

allowing the village, in its own person, to intervene. Going on tour trains him to seek the invidivual in the mass and to turn to the village as to a living being. After a few tours the vast districts, so discouraging at first because of their size and populations, fall into well-defined regions and groupings, and he can easily grasp their significant characteristics.

The territories of French West Africa then present themselves in their context: they no longer stand for a population of more than fifteen million—three times greater than that of Paris and its environs —in an area eight times the size of France: now they appear as 2,200 districts and 48,000 villages. And the villages are like islands in a sea of forest, savanna and desert, which is the bush. The 118 commandants and their heads of sub-divisions, each have their own zone of bush and their own islands. But while the bush should be as familiar to them as is the sea to a sailor, the village is not a port of call but a centre for new work. The art of going on tour involves a two-fold task: living the life of the bush and the life of the village, and the second is approached through the first.

The fatigue of the road, however great, disappears on arrival at the village. The horse whinnies, its nostrils dilating at the hope of a calabash of water and a box full of provender. The white man turns his head and his sunburnt ears towards the native huts in their ordered peace. Whether the village consists of round thatched huts or adobe cubes, however blackened the straw or crumbling the walls, every home wears the look of something laboured on to be lived in. The administrator, nevertheless, will stick to his lunatic loads: camp bed, folding table, deck-chair, hurricane lamp, food-boxes, all of them, too, in a fixed order. The camp takes shape, which is always a joy. Sometimes it looks like a little fort with a protecting wall. Usually, it is a big hut, its thick broad-eaved roof a masterpiece of plaited straw, or else two huts joined together by a tiny veranda; more huts for the servants and guards; in a corner, the bread-oven. Soon the smoke of one more fire rises in the village. The Commandant is there. It is now that he will sense if his presence is readily accepted, if the news of his coming, mysteriously sent ahead by the bush, has put him into power, and if the important things he has come for, census-taking and palaver, are going to be plain sailing.

The life of the colony is revealed to anyone who can read a budget; the life of the village is clear to him who can read a census—if the census is properly done. In most districts, it is not yet taken by names. A handful of Europeans with native clerks and the additional help of

46 FREEDOM AND AUTHORITY IN FRENCH WEST AFRICA

the teacher during the holidays, are not sufficient to make a nominal roll of some hundred thousand men every year. Things will only improve when in every village there is a former pupil of our schools charged with keeping statistical records. But even a numerical census is of great value. It is the basis of the poll-tax and the cattle-tax and of the plan of campaign for labour service. But it is not itself a fiscal operation. It is the primary instrument for measuring the demographic development of the village.

But the village demands from the administrator a more personal investigation. Who is the headman, the real headman, and what is his real name? Accuracy here is important, as will appear in the chapter on village headmen.[1] What is the nature of his power, what is his race and religion? What are the races and religions of the village? Are there wards and ward chiefs? How many heads of families, and of what sort is the family? So much for political structure.

How many births, deaths and marriages have there been in the year? Are there migrations to other villages, to neighbouring Districts and Colonies? What is the people's standard of living, what do they produce, what are the prices of the staple foods? Where are the reserve granaries? Who owns and works the land and how is it worked and owned? Is there any small local industry, any special craft? Is the market an important one? Do European or Syrian merchants come to it by lorry? Do they finance native shops and pedlars? Do they lend money to the chief and the elders, and especially money to pay tax? What is the market price of cattle and grain at the time when tax is collected, at the beginning of the year, at the gap between harvests, towards the middle of the year? What is the rate of exchange of notes in native cowrie-shell currency? Who is the money-changer and who is the money-lender in the village? So much for the economic side.

Finally, what ex-service men, what former schoolboys are there? The administrator asks to see them, without letting it be thought that he is organizing them into a private police force, at which the chief might take umbrage.

How many questions the poorest village raises! It is not easy to answer them satisfactorily. It is better not to systematize them in the

---

[1] It sometimes happens that an administrator may make a mistake even about the name of a village. Seeing a village in the distance, the administrator of the T—— Subdivision in the Niger Territory asked the interpreter its name; he misunderstood the question and replied, '*Babu mutane*' (There's nobody). In 1922 the tax list of the Subdivision, duly approved by the Governor in Council, showed the name of a new village, Babu mutane.

THE NATIVE TERRITORIES 47

form of a pre-arranged questionnaire, which would soon mean just another set of official files. The best method is a flexible one, which aims simply at putting the village at ease and arousing its interest. In order to put the village at ease, the Commandant must rigorously abstain from levying taxes and imposing fines. Such a practice should never be allowed, not only because a travelling cash box is a source of temptation but also because, at the slightest suggestion of tax-gathering, the village will shut itself up and the tour will be spoilt. Likewise the Commandant should travel with only a small staff, so that the business of feeding and lodging them does not become a burden. He should also be scrupulous in paying his own expenses and those of his staff. For these reasons also he should not send his guards or the chiefs on tour without him, as native representatives of his authority. On the contrary, he will send, in turn, his fellow-officers from headquarters who will learn from him, as the English say, to do as he does and be what he is.

Putting the village at ease is, indeed, getting it interested. In one place this may be done by collecting the children and their mothers to see if the vaccinations carried out on a recent tour have taken satisfactorily; in another, by summoning only the chiefs and elders; elsewhere by holding a court of justice, or by discussing the harvest with the heads of families. If the administrator himself is in a receptive mood he will gain the confidence of the village. Once tongues are loosened, a flood of information will pour out, which the administrator can sort out for himself.

In order to keep some record, it is only necessary to take notes in an exercise-book or note-book—one for each village—which can be passed from one administrator to another. Thus the village will have a sort of card index which, from year to year and from tour to tour, will present a picture of it drawn from life.

The administrator should not expect to discover the vital secret of the village at one stroke, nor, above all, should he look for something out of the ordinary. The key words are not riddles, but the words of common speech. The stream of everyday life is full of trivial and vital things which the observant administrator will absorb.

It will be objected that there is no time to go so deep. Thanks to a centralized administration this is true, and that is where the danger lies.

In the colonies, as in France, administration is only conceived of as exercised from a centre to the extremities. It is Napoleon's militarism. In his Saint Helena memoirs, speaking of the prefectures, he

48 FREEDOM AND AUTHORITY IN FRENCH WEST AFRICA

wrote: 'The same impulse was given at the same moment to 40 million men, and, with the help of these centres of local activity, action moved as rapidly at the extremities as at the heart itself.' But it is not only a question of giving a centrifugal impetus. Administration should also act as a centripetal force, working from the extremities to the centre. Thouret of the Constituent Assembly had grasped this when he said: 'An administration is not a good one unless it really administers. Now it cannot fulfil this object unless it is present and active at every point in its territory and can despatch every individual item of business with equal speed and efficiency.' In the same way, one of the Prefects of the Empire, de Lezay-Marnesia, insisted that sub-Prefects should travel so that they might have contact with the mayors and first-hand knowledge of the communes. Even more in the colonies, in order to influence the villages, it is necessary to get to know them by going on tour. It is not a question of settling every individual matter on the spot, but of giving to the settlement, carried out by canton and village chiefs, the imprint of a general direction, inspired by the observations of the tour.

A tour for the purpose of carrying out a census can be combined with a palaver, intended to inform the village of the intentions of the central administration. Except in special cases where it may be advisable to act unexpectedly, it is best to prepare the villages for the orders which are to be given, so that their reactions may be known in good time and they may feel that they are collaborating with government. The administrator should make no secret of the trouble and thought he has taken in thus giving them information beforehand: it may be that a school is to be opened at headquarters, or that a vaccinator is to come to the canton, or that a section of road is to be built by labour service. The tour, which is a means of getting to know the territory and collaborating with it, is for that very reason a method of administration, the essential activity of the Commandant. It is by going on tour that the Commandant puts into practice the art of native policy which binds together the colony and the territory.

IV. NATIVE POLICY

Theories and Facts

It is generally agreed that there must be a native policy and that it must be a good one. 'To initiate and maintain a good native policy is the problem to which all others are secondary.'[1]

One is tempted to bring all ideas on native policy back to the classic debate: Assimilation or Association. But in native Africa, experience is full of contradictions and compromises between these two theories. France, supposedly assimilationist, has given votes to certain Senegalese and made them eligible for election to her Parliament; but has she not at the same time respected the principle of association in safeguarding their Moslem status? England, it is said, colonizes without assimilating; but has she not anglicized the Africans of the Gold Coast in enrolling them in agricultural and marketing co-operatives, turning them into clerks at Achimota College and treating them as His Majesty's Opposition at Accra? Assimilation *or* Association? In fact one does not have to make an unconditional choice. Assimilation *and* Association, the two formulas are often combined; the dosage of each varies with the practitioner's dexterity and the temperature of events.

Harmand condemns assimilation and favours association, with some curious reservations in regard to Africa, about which he shares the feelings of his time: he believes, indeed, that Africa has no indigenous culture and therefore considers that it should be assimilated, while Asia, on the contrary, demands a policy of association. Regismanset and the author of *Réalités Coloniales*[2] taking their stand on the universalist and assimilationist character of the French genius, consider that the only policy in which France could fully exercise her distinctive methods and mastery is that of assimilation. And yet French humanism is not incompatible with a protectorate and Lyautey reigned like a prince of the blood in Morocco. In the last analysis, the only value of the policy of assimilation is the worth of

[1] Harmand, *Domination et Colonization* (Flammarion, 1910), p. 152.
[2] *Mercure de France*, 1935.

50   FREEDOM AND AUTHORITY IN FRENCH WEST AFRICA

the assimilable substance it brings to the natives;[1] while the policy of association has enduring results only in so far as it gives the native a feeling of community with the home country. On the West Coast of Africa you will not associate with cannibals unless they assimilate a different meat diet, and in the Sahel you will not assimilate the Touareg and the Moors unless you tie them down to a sedentary life —and if they don't die of it. Reality eludes the categories in which we seek to enclose it. And these same categories, which seem clear and convenient, are not or are no longer aids to knowledge; they only freeze the mind into immobility.

When the debate between Assimilation and Association ceases to be an academic dispute and becomes of administrative import, it pitches you into strange deviations. It is claimed, for example, that Assimilation leads to direct administration and Association to 'indirect rule'. And by direct administration is implied a bureaucracy modelled on that of France and centralized in Paris. 'The object to be attained in the Colonies', declared Paul Dislère, the great teacher in the École Coloniale from 1889 to 1932, 'ought to be the creation of real French administrative departments.' Let's hope it will never be attained! Happily there is a way of making Africa French without putting it into departments neatly ranged round Paris. In British Nigeria the 'indirect rule' introduced by Lord Lugard has functioned since 1900 but not without giving rise to pertinent criticisms of late. Mary Kingsley noted long ago that to govern natives by European methods, using natives to do so, is a very different proceeding from that of governing natives according to African principles. An administration which employs Africans in European offices should not be called 'indirect rule'. In Nigeria, a native employé at Lagos station gives me my ticket for Kano. A few days later, going from Kano to Zinder, I cross into the French Niger Colony which is under 'direct' administration, where the head of Magaria Subdivision requisitions camels for me from the neighbouring villages. For the same transport operation, a black man acted in European style under 'indirect rule', and a white man, under a system of direct administration, applied principles of requisitioning worthy of an African *zarki*. But political theory did not enter into it at all. It was simply the great difference between an Africa of railwaymen and an Africa of camel-drivers. And it looked as if the administration differed in its nature according

---

[1] 'We are willing to assimilate what you offer us, but not to be assimilated by you,' declared Leopold Sedan Senghor (*La communauté impériale française*, Alsatia, 1945).

NATIVE POLICY 51

to whether it had camels or a railway, and that it was African with the camels and European with the trains; and to complicate the question, it delegated an African in an 'indirect rule' colony to deal with me in European fashion, while it confided to a European in a 'direct' administration colony the task of africanizing my transport.

European methods or African principles? That is where the question should lie. But it has already passed that stage. *The time has come when African principles are no longer intrinsically native, nor European methods purely metropolitan, but both are closely mingled and profoundly modified. A new fact has come into existence—an African world which has reacted to Europe and which is creating a régime proper to itself, in administration as in everything else.* It will perhaps draw together those who believe in Assimilation and those who believe in Association, the partisans of 'direct' administration and those of 'indirect rule'. *This new African world forces us to be aware of what it wants and to devise laws that will not harm its interests.* Colonial institutions are determined by the evolution of the natives in a new African world, rather than by the theoretical conceptions of the home country.

This glance at the facts enables us to reject other classifications which insist that native policy is based on trade. There should be a policy for cocoa, coffee, bananas, cotton, cabbage-palm, manioc, groundnuts and maize. And undoubtedly one for millet which is the most important product of all, though not used for export—for it is the staple food of most of the producers. There are few African territories where the people only grow one staple food crop. Even where this is supposed to be the case, as in Senegal with its groundnuts, they have a fairly complex agricultural economy. Senegal's principal export is groundnuts, but millet is also grown there.

Some writers would invoke the support of ethnology and base native policy on religions and races. But consider the following table:

Approximate distribution of the native population of French West Africa according to tribal groups and religions in the middle of 1936.

1. Distribution according to tribal groups (in thousands):

Moors	450
Tuareg	270
Fulani (Peuls, Foula, Fulbe)	1,965
Mossi	1,460
Bambara and Mandingo	1,290
Malinke	595
Wolof	630

52 FREEDOM AND AUTHORITY IN FRENCH WEST AFRICA

Senufo	680
Toucouleur	270
Susu	255
Marka	320
Diola	115
Serer	305
Habbe and Dogon	185
Songhai	140
Kissi	140
Anyi and Baule	490
Dan and Gouro	265
Kwa-Kwa	140
Krumen	380
Lobi	210
Djedje	390
Fon and Aja	260
Bariba	240
Nago	140
Djerma	160
Hausa	530
Others	2,715
Total	14,990

2. Distribution according to religions (in thousands):

Pagans	8,150
Moslems	6,250
Christians	350
Total	14,750

As far as religions are concerned, is one to judge according to the total number of the faithful, taking French West Africa as a whole? There are 6,250,000 Moslem or Moslemized Africans against 8,150,000 pagans and 350,000 Christians. As far as tribes are concerned, they number at least 25, from the Nago, 140,000 strong in Dahomey, to the Peul (Fulani), 1,965,000 of whom are scattered throughout French West Africa. And one also finds two and a half million Africans who are not or are no longer members of any well-defined tribe. Is one to commit the political mistake of putting one religion or tribe before the others? And if one wishes to follow a special policy in respect of each of them, how is one to set about doing so in one and the same country where they live side by side when they are not intermingled?

Instead of arguing in broad terms, let us turn to one territory. Here is the Bobo *Cercle* on the Ivory Coast. It exports 8,000 metric

NATIVE POLICY 53

tons of groundnuts in the shell, 1,000 tons of shea nuts, 50 tons of cotton. It produces millet, *fonio*—a grain still smaller than millet yams, peas, tomatoes, vegetable oils and fats for the vital needs of its 300,000 inhabitants. It has 2,133 Catholics, 4,470 Protestants, 5,300 Moslems and the rest pagans. The census distinguishes, as far as tribes are concerned, 10,000 Bambara, 50 Baule, 385 Ble, 9,113 Bobo Dyula, 28,000 Bobo Fing, 6,000 Bobo Wule, 5,000 Bolon, 150 Dafing, 41,000 Diola, 4,470 Dorosse, 39,600 Gouin, 350 Hausa, 16,000 Karaboro, 3,000 Kouwno, 2 Krumen, 1,000 Marka, 2,200 Mossi, 13,000 Nanerge, 777 Natioro, 21,000 Nienege, 3,400 Wara, 2,500 Fulani, 7,600 Sambla, 7,000 Sano, 1 Senegalese, 21,700 Senufo, 5,000 Tagwa, 5,400 Tiefo, 46 Toucouleur, 11,000 Toussian, 25,700 Turka, 25,000 Vige. The first thing that strikes one is the presence of elements whose small numbers indicate either that they are foreign or that they are in the process of disappearing. The 385 Ble, for example, are in process of disappearing. The 2,500 Fulani, the 2,200 Mossi have slipped into the Bobo *Cercle* by infiltration. The 50 Baule, the 350 Hausa, the 46 Toucouleur, the 2 Krumen and the one and only Senegalese have still more obviously settled there very recently. And yet they matter to the country all the same. And a good native policy must have a care for them and not reserve its entire activity for the strong, autochthonous groupings. A patchwork of small tribes has as much importance as a great conglomeration. They are all human beings. Is it quite certain that the clear-cut demarcations which may have existed formerly between Bambara and Bobo, Dyula and Gouin and Senufo are still valid? These peoples have been thrown together, have intermarried. A native policy swayed by the notion of mass and race would get further and further away from the complex local reality, and, instead of taking the territories in a firm grasp, would lose itself in over-simplification and abstraction. The case of the one and only Senegalese is interesting. There you have a man no longer designated by his tribe, but by his colony. We are not told what tribe in Senegal he belongs to, Serer, Wolof or Lebu. That he comes from the Colony of Senegal is enough to give him some sort of status, and for native policy to know whom it is dealing with. He is not a *deraciné* from a small, isolated Africa; in Bobo *Cercle* he is a son of the mother colony of all the colonies of the Federation. He is settled in Bobo as he might be elsewhere, as a man of the new African world that has got beyond race, where natives of all races give life to the colonial structure and break it open from within.

54   FREEDOM AND AUTHORITY IN FRENCH WEST AFRICA

It may be said that the example of Bobo is badly chosen, and that there do exist mono-racial *cercles*, Ouagadougou for instance. In Ouagadougou *Cercle*, it is true, there is a *bloc* of 347,400 Mossi in the midst of a population of 469,000 inhabitants. But the minorities are not negligible: 42,000 Gurunsi, 30,000 Kassena, 14,000 Nankana, 16,000 Yarsi, 9,000 Fulani, and there are fragmentary tribes as well: Bussanse, Dagari.

Let us recognize then that native policy ought to be based on men as they are, in the countries where they live. It should constantly adapt itself to them and not attempt to reduce them to some major category—economic, religious or racial. If they grow cotton to sell and millet to eat, native policy will be as much concerned with trade as with food supply. And if they grow millet on the slopes, it will know that they are not exactly the same as they would be if they grew it on level ground. Native policy will go with them wherever they go to worship—to church, temple, mosque or sacred grove. It will follow them in their racial groups and in their racial mixtures. It will go with them on their marches and migrations, on the intercolonial roads, through all the countries of the new African world. It will show concern for the isolated individual as well as interest in the homogeneous group. It will always seek out the human beings, and it is in order to find them the more surely that it first studies their countries. *Native policy does not fit the countries into a theory; it simply sees in them the territorial basis where its action can be de-limited and verified.* It does not express itself in formulas. It is a state of mind which permeates every institution. *The rule of action of native policy, applicable to every country, is to organize and give life to public authority over the natives by recognizing that they have rights and by caring for their interests.*

EFFECTS OF METHODS OF CONQUEST

Public authority in French West Africa is still bound up with the way the military conquest of the countries was carried out. And French native policy may be explained historically by the so-called 'bit by bit' method. This method has been derided, but it did force the colonial generals to seek the maximum results in Africa with the minimum of means from Europe. The numerical weakness of their troops impelled them to discover in the country to be conquered the resources necessary for completing the conquest: man-power by recruiting natives, intellectual power by studying the populations and

NATIVE POLICY

getting used to them. Action undertaken in this way is patient, but solid. It raises up native allies. Diplomacy camps with the column. Barnavaux was a leader who knew how to negotiate and how to govern. Conquest became organization on the march. 'If, when taking a village', said Lyautey, 'one is thinking of the market that one is going to set up there, one does not take it in the same way.' Colonial warfare in West Africa in the nineteenth century, far from giving lessons to Europe, was much behind it; instead of moving great massed armies and proceeding by extermination and prestige, it worked covertly to bring about a political domination acceptable to the countries. Thus in the Soudan, Borgnis-Desbordes, Archinard and Trentinian never had the strength of a brigade, but they conquered the Soudan in the process of organizing it. Sparing of blood and money, such a conquest was honourable in the sense that it did not affect the land. It did not exterminate the natives; it has not despoiled them of their fields.

The importance for native policy of this 'bit by bit' method appears with fresh significance when one thinks of the Italian expedition against Ethiopia in 1935. 400,000 soldiers and militarized labourers, we are told, were brought to open the way to Addis-Abbaba, and thirty-one million lire were spent from 1935 to 1937. For the first time, colonial warfare was a projection of European warfare on to the African plane. I wrote at the time that what Italy called a colonial expedition was in fact an act of secession from Europe, and this is what I meant: Up till then, no colonizing country was ever totally engaged in any colonial war. Neither the political régime nor the economic régime of the colonizing country was staked on a colonial operation. Italy changed all that. To bring down the Negus, Mussolini socialized Rome. To send troops and material to the Generalissimo, Marshal Badoglio, he decreed a forced loan, blocked Italian assets abroad and plunged deeper into autarchy. The defeat of Adowa in the time of Crispi did not have any serious consequences for the lives of the Italians. The technical difficulties of the Italian victory in 1935, just as much as the resulting political tension between Italy on the one hand and England and France on the other, impelled Fascism to gird up all its forces and all those of the Italian country. Far from being a 'small colonial expedition', as the majority of French journalists called it, it was a total war and one that had more repercussions on the colonizing power than on the colonized. The Negus was defeated and had to flee, but the Italian bourgeoisie and nineteenth-century liberalism had preceded him into disaster. An important

56 FREEDOM AND AUTHORITY IN FRENCH WEST AFRICA

change was introduced into the colonial relationship between Africa and Europe. It was no longer a question of a European nation obtaining a colonial gain in Africa with little risk, by means of a localized military action carried out by specialists; on the contrary, the Italian nation had to develop to the uttermost its own political, economic and cultural régime, even to the extent of endangering the peace of Europe. Quite apart from any question of justice and morality, no conquest of an African territory had ever involved such a political upheaval in a metropolitan country in Europe.

'The Way Faidherbe Worked'

French conquest, infinitely wiser, and largely a sequel to exploration, foreshadowed a native policy that the Africans have been able to accept.

Even the process of conquest itself displayed qualities of individual research and critical understanding derived from the spirit of exploration, and thus the native policy of the conquerors appeared not as a Machiavellian tyranny but rather as a collaboration with the indigenous peoples in opening up a new world. It was a policy which, coming to birth in the very hour of conquest, and shaped by the special character of the country, turned at the same time towards the ideal of the French Revolution, Liberty, Equality, Fraternity. It has been said that these principles cannot be applied to colonies and that, though they figure on official letter-heads and public buildings, they have been belied in action. This is not true. In Senegal, the mother colony of French West Africa, a colonial governor successfully carried out a policy of liberation of the slaves, education of the natives and fraternity between races. M. A. Villard, keeper of the archives at Dakar, who is researching into the sources of African history, has described the work of Faidherbe.[1]

'With a few poorly equipped offices, this man succeeded in making a colony, in giving it a stable organization, in preparing for it a future which was to have decisive effects on the whole of French West Africa; his amazing achievement compels even the most cautious to regard it as in the nature of a miracle, and in truth, history can show very few miracles. Faidherbe's own vigorous personality does not entirely account for it; his training, his earlier experience before he came to Senegal, the methods he used, provided an essential supplement to his natural gifts.

[1] *Bulletin d'informations et de renseignements d'A.O.F.* No. 205, 24 Oct. 1938.

'His statues and portraits have made everyone familiar with the stern features, the be-spectacled eyes, the severe lines of the military cap, which make up that rather forbidding countenance, which the formidable moustache does little to improve. Thus there soon arose the legend of Faidherbe, the Polytechnic student, the arid intellectual, the mathematician, the narrow logician, the stern administrator with his rigid principles. I confess that I prefer the gentler, more benevolent qualities of Faidherbe, the old senator, sick, may be, but with a lively mind and a quick intelligence; the veteran colonial, rather dis-illusioned and still more disappointed by the war of 1870; constant in his devotion to mathematics and logic, with a mind of great subtlety tempered by a profound understanding of the land and of men and by real kindness of heart. When, as an engineer officer, he went to Dabou with the Baudin expedition, he doubtless took with him all the necessary treatises on ballistics and fortification, the few regulation textbooks which counted for something in those days; but what he carried in his own head was more valuable: unforgettable memories of the Antilles during the rising of 1848; the hardships of the Algerian campaign, which left its mark, not only on his soul but on his body, the cruel legacy of the snows of Kabyle which had twisted his limbs with rheumatism. He had been deeply affected by the struggles in Guadaloupe in which negroes, mulattoes and creoles took arms against one another. It seemed to him that the cause lay in a failure of mutual understanding, due to lack of education and dis-trust of out-dated or vicious economic systems. Thus he was led to consider seriously the intricate problems of immigration and mixed marriages and the important question of education.

'In Algeria he learned something of the Islamic institutions of the Malekite order; the working of the "Arab centres" then in process of expansion, inclined him to political methods which were both firm and flexible and relied rather on knowing and making contact with the people than on ill-considered military actions.

'Fate led him to a territory recently Islamized through contact with the Berbers who had been converted at an earlier date and were full of missionary fervour; in this territory there was a mulatto com-munity, in close and constant touch with the African peoples, which could be skilfully made use of. Faidherbe, disgusted with the official colonization policy which was being pursued only half-heartedly in Algeria, set himself to improve the land, with the aid of the native inhabitants; took stock of the actual situation of the people and the country and dealt with them with all the skill and wisdom he had

58 FREEDOM AND AUTHORITY IN FRENCH WEST AFRICA

acquired in the hard school of defeat and failure—without illusions but also without distaste.

'Dabou cannot have been a very encouraging scene for him. All his life he retained a dislike for the South Coast. The miserable trading posts of Bassam and Assinie, and the unhealthy climate alike distressed him. The Ministry of Marine had failed, more or less completely, to colonize the coastal peoples, through lack of funds, energy and political sense, as well as through lack of support from Gorée and St. Louis. Faidherbe concluded, therefore, no doubt too hastily, that the peoples of the territory were uninteresting. The future proved him wrong, but it was the only mistake he made. It shows how, owing to lack of information or personal dislike, a man like Faidherbe could under-estimate some of the most important territories, from the point of view of population and production, that we possess.

'He was infinitely better prepared to like and understand the northern territories; there he was following the trail of mediaeval Europe and of the trading companies. The past as well as the present came to his assistance, and Faidherbe cannot be separated either from his predecessors or from his collaborators.

'He included among his predecessors many who were long before him in time. He studied, even if he did not believe, the most horrific stories of the ancient voyages of discovery, the simple-minded records of religious orders, the fraudulent accounts of the companies. All these he passed through the crucible of a ruthless criticism.

'He divined the bonds which, in the middle ages, united the Berber and the negro worlds. Timbuctoo, Ghana, Mali, lured him on, not in order to fill his pockets with legendary gold or to give his name to some discovery, but to find a solution to the ancient mystery of the mediaeval Soudan. He had a great opinion of Caillié and Molhen. He distrusted the coast towns, the muddy estuaries where trading posts were established for more or less legitimate traffic, and where there was no prosperity; he sought the interior, the sources, for logical as much as administrative reasons. He always wanted to know where men, ideas or rivers came from.

'He knew that, nearer to his own day, many men of great gifts had been worn out in Senegal, and had been left unused without being able to give what they were capable of.

'The second Empire, whatever its faults, at least may have the credit for being less extravagant in the way of transfers than the previous régime, and for appointing substitutes. Faidherbe did not despise the experience of his predecessors: for him Roger, Bonet,

NATIVE POLICY 59

Protet, Baudin, were neither cowards nor fools; Duranton, himself, though a poor administrator, was noteworthy for his writings. Nearly every Senegalese question had been passed in review before Faidherbe's time, but decisive political action was needed to effect a solution.

'Faidherbe retained what came to be the geographical framework of the future colony, taking the Senegal River as the boundary as far as Falémé, joining Upper Falémé and Upper Gambia to Upper Casamance, and securing the coast from St. Louis to Cape Roxo. The trading posts at Guinea and elsewhere Faidherbe regarded merely as bases and possible bridgeheads for advance towards the Soudan: he had no great belief in their economic future. If he did little to advance it, neither did he impede it, and he successfully defended French rights against the British and Portuguese in this respect.

'He had an exceptionally fine collaborator in Pinet-Laprade, whose tact and skill persuaded his chief to extend the range of his attention beyond his prime objective, the Upper River, and include the sector of Gorée and Guinea. Pinet-Laprade, half-soldier and half-sailor, built forts and explored the estuaries; he was the real founder of Dakar, Casamance and Guinea, but he died too soon to see the development of these colonies. And there were all the others, notable explorers who traversed the regions bordering on Senegal—Mauritania, Bambouck, Kaarta, Bélédougou—and the young men who got themselves killed up and down the country. Ignoring official distinctions, Faidherbe set himself to extinguish old quarrels; he did even better and gained the confidence of the local inhabitants by giving responsible positions to young Senegalese officers; Descemet, who died at Medina, remains a symbol of that devoted generation.

'He did not ignore the opinions of the trading community, nor those of the clergy and the civil authorities, but he did not hesitate to rebuke publicly and violently those who felt impelled, for the sake of private interests, to impede his activity; the speeches he made at banquets and prize-givings are significant in this connection. He had to have assistants, and permanent assistants, and he sought them among the indigenous population, or rather he sought to make the whole population co-operate with him in his task. He had a great belief in the importance of office work; reports from the bush or from native informants, when studied and reflected on calmly in the fort at St. Louis, would ripen into sane and sensible orders and practicable plans. He had no use for red tape, for notes and memoranda, for masterly inactivity. Exacting in matters of discipline himself, he did

60 FREEDOM AND AUTHORITY IN FRENCH WEST AFRICA

not scruple to ignore the regulations devised by stay-at-home officials in the Ministry of Marine. The bridge at Guet N'Dar (now the Servatius Bridge) was built at little expense and opened to traffic the very day he received the minister's despatch authorizing the construction to be carried out the following year. He never sacrificed action in field-tours and reconnaissance to paper work.

'He soon saw that Europeans did not stand the climate and could only be relied on to furnish temporary staff. He therefore aimed at drawing his collaborators from the soldiers, traders and other permanent residents. Thus he was led to study at close quarters the peoples of Senegal and their languages and customs, and he urged his officers to do the same. He signed his own name to the notes published in the official journal. All his writings are concerned with Senegal or West Africa, and he expressed himself equally well in his learned studies of the Fulani and the Cayor and in short popular papers written for the general public and for schools.

'His intensive study of the country led him to believe that the Christian mulatto population, which had long been French speaking, was in many respects European in outlook, while at the same time in close touch with the indigenous people, speaking their language and having a considerable influence on them. There is no doubt that, in Faidherbe's time, a mulatto family trading in St. Louis or Gorée would have numerous clients scattered the length of the river or along the Little Coast, that it would have former slaves freed or working for wages, that it would carry on its trade humanely and would have resources at its disposal which the Government could not ignore.

'Faidherbe knew also that among the native peoples, however backward they might seem to be, were active and intelligent men, loyal to France, and able to form a body of leaders, such as was essential for native administration.

'He had quickly estimated the average value of the European staff at his disposal. As a result of the Thévenard incident in 1848, the events of Bakel in 1829, and later the Cayor question, he was able to foresee, and subsequently to verify, the wisdom of the principle that the chief officer at a station should confine himself to controlling, administering, and sending in careful reports, and should not engage in questions of policy. The "Arab Bureaux" did not seem likely to be successful in Senegal, though their methods and their spirit were adopted. Faidherbe's subordinates did not always know the country as well as their chief did, and moreover, there were too many of them.

'The two tendencies already described account for the two-fold system of education initiated by Faidherbe: on the one hand, a classical, Christian education closely modelled on that of France, preparing the best pupils for further studies in France, while fitting the others for subordinate posts in the Administration and in business, fields which were quickly invaded by the mulattoes and certain African elements; on the other hand, a purely secular education—intended to avoid alienating the Moslems, designed to train the sons of chiefs and, to a lesser extent, workers and clerks. For girls of good family, religious education intended to train them as mistresses of households or companions, after the French provincial fashion; for others training in household work. All very fine schemes.

'A study of the results brings us to the heart of the struggle in which Faidherbe, all his life, was involved: the continual conflict between his reason, and the actions forced on him by his ruthless apprehension of the facts. He did indeed get results. The school for the sons of chiefs provided Senegal with some good chiefs, some good interpreters and some fine examples of treachery. The education reserved for the sons of Europeans, the children of colonial families and a few selected Africans, can now be judged; it did in fact produce a brilliant generation which gave to commerce, to the administration and to the army, in Dakar as at Gorée and Rufisque, recruits of undeniably high quality; on the other hand it created in Senegal, among both men and women, that shocking mentality, typical of the French nineteenth-century middle classes, the disastrous consequences of which are being experienced, even in France, to-day. The towns took on the aspect of French *sous-préfectures* and the inhabitants of them were greatly inferior to their fathers in knowledge of the native and of the native territories. Faidherbe, in his later years, was clearly disappointed by the enormous change which his educational system had made in the inhabitants of the colony. They were less useful in the fields of political and commercial activity, and while they had gained a European education and a knowledge of French parliamentary legislation they had lost effectiveness as regards native policy and affairs.

'As far as the native African peoples were concerned, the results were better. But Faidherbe was always a prey to doubts. The conversion to Christianity of the young Moslems of Cayor or Tonta Toro was not to be thought of and the Governor knew better than anyone the qualities and defects of Islam. He tried to Europeanize them within the setting of Islam, but he was continually frustrated. Though he succeeded in establishing the cultivation of cash crops,

62 FREEDOM AND AUTHORITY IN FRENCH WEST AFRICA

such as groundnuts, or in developing stock breeding, he never succeeded in changing the customary behaviour and the status of women. His millet-flour mill at St. Louis fell into disuse. The system exasperated him. Islam preserved peace at Cayor, where the pagan *tiédos* maltreated the unfortunate *marabout* peasants, and provoked war on the River, where the pastoralists and merchants were continually threatened by Moors and Toucouleurs. Either way, it caused suffering. However, according to the opportunities which offered, in one way or another, he made whatever sacrifice the well-being of the country demanded.

'He was conscious of the imminence of two powerful factors which were destined to destroy all his work for the education, assimilation and utilization of local human resources.

'As conquest and pacification progressed, hundreds of negroes from the newly acquired territories poured into Gorée, St. Louis and Rufisque and settled there. Gradually a native *élite* would emerge which, by the nature of things, would out-number and surpass in influence the mulatto society which increased more slowly and had been reduced by disease. The conquest of the colonies of the South, moreover, which marked the political apogee of Senegal, was to deliver a crushing blow to that society by greatly diminishing its resources; the years preceding 1900 saw the establishment of great colonial companies which restricted the number and the activities of private traders and seriously depleted their financial resources. Their descendants took Government posts or entered the liberal professions or left the country—thus greatly reducing the influence of that section of the population.

'Military and political developments were equally distressing to the old Governor: the Senegal River, which he had cared for most of all the African countryside, was superseded by the Niger, which he had longed to see. Tied to his chair, Faidherbe, by means of an admirable letter, wrested from the Senate credits for the Kayes—Bamoko railway, thus destroying his town of Medina; he prepared the way for the Dakar—Niger line and the decline of St. Louis. Everywhere, at Thiés, at Kaolack, at Ziguinchor, on the site of his wretched forts, a mushroom growth of towns was to spring up, rivalling St. Louis which was thus vanquished by the man who had most loved it. Faidherbe who, more than all other governors, had earned the name of "Borom N'Dar", was the one who prepared the way for the decline of that city.

'Everything Faidherbe did to achieve certain ends was in fact diminished or destroyed when those ends were attained. He forged a magnificent instrument, a mother-colony, but the daughters grew up faster. St. Louis, mother of three colonies: Mauritania, Soudan, Niger; Gorée, mother of the three southern colonies: Guinea, the Ivory Coast, Dahomey.

'True, his successors reached Timbuctoo and saw the Niger, but the colonies of mangroves and coconuts, of palm-oil and cocoa, the colonies of estuaries and lagoons, which Faidherbe never loved, have far outstripped by their wealth the country of sand, groundnuts and millet.

'Because of his wisdom and his sincerity he often had the courage to act against the dictates of his feelings. He was a student in the 1830's, and captivated by the notion of liberty, but more than once he doubted whether the rapid emancipation of conquered peoples was really a good thing, when it filled the prisons with vagrants, thieves and prostitutes collected from the streets of St. Louis; he respected the forms of native society, but he did not hesitate to liberate slaves and semi-slaves when some petty king of Sine or Cayor abused the rights he laid claim to.

'Uncertainty, suffering; the attacks of those whom he most cherished—the merchants of St. Louis who accused him of hampering trade with the Moors when in fact he was preserving them from a raid which would have destroyed them; attacks from Moslems who objected to education, attacks from Christians who criticized his native policy as showing too much deference to Islam; the chilliness of conservative-minded colleagues who preferred the days of paperwork without action. It must be admitted that he received more praise after death than during his life.

'He knew how to adapt, and how to adapt himself; he suffered for the sake of Senegal and its future. He took measures which were bound to destroy the present achievement in order to bring to birth something greater to take its place. St. Louis, in its decline, could be proud of Bamako, of Kayes, of the Soudan railway; Gorée, dying itself, was the begetter of Dakar and the strident clamour of the southern wharves.

'Faidherbe saw things on a grand scale and saw them in their true proportions, even if his beloved Senegal had to suffer for it. He loved the Wolof, but half at least of his writings were devoted to describing the Mandingo, Serer, Sarakolles, Toucouleur, Diola—whom he had made Senegalese.

'For the government of the territories born from the colony which his methods had created, he left as legacy simply his method—which

64   FREEDOM AND AUTHORITY IN FRENCH WEST AFRICA

may be expressed in one word: knowledge. He made it clear that for his own sake and for the sake of his office a man must submit himself to the experience of his predecessors when it is well founded, to the logic of facts, when it is irrefutable, to a knowledge of the country, when he is sure that he has it.

'He had his disciples. On 17 January 1918, a captain in the Colonial Infantry, Governor-General in civil life,[1] addressed a letter to a Minister for Colonies in which he explained that he could no longer remain in office to carry out measures which he considered, from his own knowledge and experience, to be vexatious and humiliating. After which he departed and was killed on a road in Champagne where a war was going on.

'One day in 1858, a governor of Senegal, a brilliant army officer, wrote to a Minister of Marine to offer his resignation on account of a measure which would have re-established *de facto* slavery: this officer spoke in very apt terms of peoples whom he knew only by hearsay, but who, he said "could produce on their own soil, without the pressure of unjust and inhuman methods, enough to repay on a generous scale those European peoples who are willing to take an interest in them and protect them".

'Though their circumstances were different, these two spoke the same language. As a result of thought and action, study and observation—on their own part and through their fellow-workers, they knew what they were talking about. They did not claim to be infallible but, for the sake of the truth as they saw it, they staked their lives and their careers, and God knows, they loved their work! They felt responsible for their own view of things, and, as honourable men, they were ready to pay the price. They have been rewarded by some hundredweight of wretchedly sculptured marble and bronze. Have they also, perhaps, earned the praise of some generations of colonials and colonized? That praise would be still more precious if it were founded on a real appreciation, not merely of the results achieved, the reports published, the cities founded, but of the sufferings of mind and heart endured by two men who agonized to achieve justice. For them, colonizing meant giving their whole hearts to the tasks they undertook, and being guided in everything not by pure reason alone but by wide vision, by the impulse of the spirit, by those fundamental and indescribable human qualities which, if they are crowned by any measure of success, are recognized as the marks of genius.'

The Faidherbe régime came to an end with the war of 1914, but we

[1] Joost van Vollenhoven.

NATIVE POLICY

have to continue his work. This was expressed by one of our colleagues at the time of the inauguration of the *Syndicat National des Administrateurs des Colonies* in 1937.[1]

'We are making a preposterous claim—namely, to do, quite simply, what always needed to be done. You will understand at once the righteous indignation or the shocked silence of the patent-medicine vendors, the pocket Machiavellis of the colonial racket. The game is up if people go in for doing what they say and saying what they do. Let us make ourselves clear. Our rustic simplicity does not go so far as to maintain, in order to embellish our cause, that actions have always been opposed to principles, and that the progress of the natives and the prosperity of the colonies have never been more than the theme of impassioned speeches, the idyllic stage-set, back of which the darkest tragedies were enacted. No one appreciates more than we do the greatness of what has been accomplished, and the generous tradition which, in the face of the immense difficulties created by a cruel climate, and poverty-stricken peoples—and in spite of mistakes and misdeeds, has built up the most humane of all colonial empires. Many of our fellows have given their health and their lives to this achievement, and we also have chosen to dedicate to it the best that is in us. For we know that it is already moving, and will increasingly move in the very direction which is every day officially proclaimed. After all, speeches are not entirely fruitless, and it is not true that several generations of men, or even one, can be continuously and systematically opposed to the ideas they profess. In the end faith comes to those who go on praying.

'Shall we then merely have added one more voice to the academic chorus? Shall we have dug up the battle-axe only to tilt at phantoms —or windmills? We do not think so. For in order to go forward it is not enough to face in the right direction. It is necessary to move and (at least we should like to) as quickly as possible. We know the magnitude of the tasks to be carried out, the poverty of the means at our disposal, the cost of all the energy, the good will, the wealth which will still have to be flung into this vast crucible. We want the colonies to profit by it, and our only aim is to ensure a wise use of our resources in this enterprise.

'In this connection our determination is not without value. For even if the general direction is in line with our wishes, there is still too much opposition and lack of understanding, too many selfish interests threatening to compromise or postpone results.

[1] *Bulletin des Administrateurs des Colonies*, No. 2, April 1937.

66   FREEDOM AND AUTHORITY IN FRENCH WEST AFRICA

'And if we are qualified by our colonial experience to make a useful contribution towards clearing the way, we might say that we also have a right to do so: the right which any craftsman has to protect the work to which he has dedicated his powers, and to see that the best possible use is made of his labour. And finally, have we not the greatest possible professional interest? An interest which touches our inmost conscience?

'Every one of our fellow-workers in the bush has at one time or another detected a discrepancy between the moderation officially required in the collection of tax, and the estimate made of his professional "output" when the total has been added up; between paternal pronouncements about the sanctity of food crops and some order—originating from an unknown source—that they are to be suddenly abandoned in favour of a more profitable cash crop; between the principles of free labour—enunciated with great solemnity—and certain "voluntary" recruitments for the benefit of enterprises whose importance is perhaps hardly worth such sacrifices. This discrepancy has sometimes caused a certain uneasiness, a sensation of moral discomfort born of uncertainty as to motives. Our aim is to destroy this shadow. To know the reason for what is being done, and the relation between the particular interests which one is serving and the general good: will not this integrity in action make ours the finest and the most thrilling of all professions?'

There can be no Native Policy without Residencies

What really threatens our native policy is not its principles but the bureaucratic centralization which prevents their being tried out experimentally. There is no surer means of making native policy sterile and reducing it to an inoperative collection of formulas than to transform administrators into bureaucrats and suppress the centre of administrative knowledge of the country, the workshop of the territorial job: the Residency.

Once, when travelling, I went into a Residency towards evening to pass the night there. It was bereft of its administrator and abandoned. On the pretext that communications had improved, headquarters had decreed that it was unnecessary and had closed it, tacking its district of 40,000 souls on to a distant *Cercle*. I have never realized the art of native policy more clearly than I did there in that empty workshop. That art is not an abstract thing, and it needs a home. This particular Residency was a dwelling of crude brick and adobe like all those

NATIVE POLICY

which the administrators got the villages to put up for them from the common clay of the country in the old days of the Niger and the Upper Volta. Sometimes their position in the plain is marked by a group of trees lining the approach as to a castle. But their finest site is on a sandy dune, a laterite knoll or the edge of a geological fault, where they dominate the sweep of thorny steppe under that ashy shimmer which is characteristic of the Soudan. They are all alike in their fortified but hospitable air, in their interior geometry which I always find restful to the mind, and in the secret harmony which unites them with the country and with our art. What a joy it is, after a tour, to come back to the shelter of that overhanging roof! They symbolize the presence of the public authority, the tenure of the administration. They bear a name that exactly defines the essential condition of authority and command: Residency. Residence is necessary. The Commandant is above all the Resident. His residence consists in working over the country, tour by tour, and coming back to the home where he works out a policy suited to the people.

In that former Residency where my nocturnal encampment disturbed the bats, how could I not be haunted by this necessity for a real presence? Census registers and recruiting lists, tax and expense accounts, court records. Law Digests, volumes of the *Journal Official*, the current files and diaries, had all been taken away, far from the district, to that headquarters where everything was centralized. What was missing, however, was not so much the apparatus, as the exercise of the art. What had been broken was the invisible thread, the nerve which linked the Residency to the villages. What had happened to the villages? The art of administering them was simple but it needed a house inhabited by a responsible man. That art is the opposite of tyranny; it needs no spectacular display of force; to judge by the number of round huts that lifted their pointed straw roofs behind the Residency, fifteen guards had sufficed to police a district of 40,000 inhabitants. No parades of speechifying, no striking of impressive attitudes. No pedantry either, but action; the working out each day of a sort of rule of three: to give life to public authority over the people by recognizing their rights and serving their interests. For there is no real authority except one which sets itself bounds and derives its own efficacy from the rights and interests of the men whom it rules.

What were the rights in this district, and where did the interests lie? It was for the district to say, but there was no longer a Resident to ask it questions. It had doubtless known, in the Commandants

68   FREEDOM AND AUTHORITY IN FRENCH WEST AFRICA

who succeeded each other at the Residency, good administrators, and less good—the best of them would be a prey to fatigue, losing their tempers towards the end of a tour when they were waiting for their relief; but these vicissitudes could not do the harm that was finally accomplished by a fatal centralization. It now had a road that brought it within five hours by car from the *Cercle*, but even if it had earned enough money to possess cars and take advantage of this progress, it would nevertheless have suffered from its abandonment: no practitioner recorded its rights any longer or gave ear to its interests. The peasant concerned about his field, in which perhaps collective property and private property overlapped; the married woman about her dowry—and her own earnings; the village chief about the scale of taxation; all these people should have been able to go to the Residency or consult the Resident on tour and say: This is what I have come about—see that I get my due.

And the greatest of all rights, the most fruitful of all interests—liberty—is in danger of disappearing. It is in isolated villages that the press-gang men disobey regulations and load lorries with workers hired dirt cheap for timber cutting in the South. It is in neglected regions that the peasant is left defenceless against secret slavers. For him his primary right is that of not being torn from his village, of not being the victim of an illicit labour draft which would transport him into the province of the Niger Office.

The Resident exercises harsh powers. He can summon men who evade census, tax-paying, labour service, and if they persist in disobeying he arrests them under the Native Status Disciplinary Code, and sentences them to a few francs' fine or a few days' imprisonment. He is equally hard on those who spread false news, who support the intrigues of deposed chiefs, who revive religious or racial hatred, who, in fine, disturb public order. He levies in men and money and labour the district's contribution towards the 12,000 *tirailleurs*, the 175 million francs of poll-tax and cattle-tax, and the 21 million days of labour service that all the 118 *cercles* together provide for French West Africa every year.

His powers have often appeared, not only contrary to the forms and the principle of liberty, but also mutually contradictory because of the divergent actions they produce. Thus he will enforce disarmament in his district, and destroy spears and bows, while at the same time he sends the young men into the army where they will be trained to handle machine-guns; he will eradicate serfdom within families, but, at the demand of notables and elders, he will enforce orders prohibiting vagrancy against young men who want to spend their private earnings away from the traditional discipline of the community. He will make mistakes from time to time, but things can always be put right if he himself is in the district to try out the regulations on the spot, to adjust the methods of keeping order, and explore the conditions of liberty; if he is there to protect the people against excessive taxation, forced labour, recruitment, requisitions—all the weapons which he has to handle in such a way as to administer without causing hurt.

It is only by living the life of the country that he can make it both orderly and free. He will learn that the most positive rights of those he administers are not always written down in the regulations but are embodied in their daily lives; that some of them are in process of disappearing and others in process of development, and that the latter are no less important and require no less discernment to give them form. He will discover that one only organizes liberty by re-creating the country itself. There is no territory, however poor and awkward, that does not deserve such care. None that ought to be abandoned or neglected for the benefit of other regions, supposedly richer, or of so-called imperial plans, devised in Paris by the great concerns for whom the colony is a market and a field of enterprise. To re-create the country is not to turn it upside down by regrouping the villages, when the particular nature of the land has put them in hamlets, or by arranging them around the Residency or along the main roads. It is first of all to leave them where they are and stimulate their motives for living, which are to be found as much in food crops as in local arts.

This native policy should be thoroughly understood; it does not imply inaction or non-interference, but rather intelligent observation. It does not offer to the administrator the soothing suggestion that he should entrench himself in his district as in an independent territory without troubling about established rules. He is well aware that the district cannot develop its own value independently of the colony. As an official he is conscious that he is both restrained and sustained by the bonds of his office and the official hierarchy. Far from paying no heed to the regulations, he has tried them out experimentally and has observed their impact on native interests from the inside, in a thousand individual cases. He does not act simply as an executive engaged in implementing the orders received from the bureaucracy. He is a man of creative imagination and of action, whose district is at once his base and his reagent, being regarded as nothing else but

70 FREEDOM AND AUTHORITY IN FRENCH WEST AFRICA

the environment favourable to the African, the framework within which he is revealed not as an abstraction but as a man. And the administrator, the Commandant, the Resident has to inform headquarters of the system of rights—the Law—that he and this flesh-and-blood man are making between them and of the interests they handle together.

It is thus that a real native policy comes into being. It depends on a territorial administration able to test out in the districts the regulations devised in a European office. It develops by means of experiments, the results of which can be scrutinized and compared in research departments. The Government at Dakar and the Ministry in Paris should play the part of research laboratories and hand on their attempts at a synthesis to the Residencies where they may be tried out experimentally and corrected. The territories will develop themselves, by means of successive adjustments, in an atmosphere of freedom. The art of native policy will regulate, with gradually increasing precision, the relations between the rights and interests of the administration and those of the native peoples; in this way it will build the new world of Africa.

V. THE NATIVE CHIEFS

STRAW CHIEFS AND CHIEFS OF THE LAND

WHEN I was head of a subdivision on the Upper Volta, I went on tour in the first months of my stay, and landed unexpectedly in a distant village, little visited. The Chief gave me a good reception. I came back there two years later, at the end of my tour, and had a still better reception. The Chief, however, did not seem to me to be the same man. I had before me an old man, while it was a young man who had received me the first time, and I recognized him, standing behind the old man. I asked the two of them why the chieftainship of the village had passed from the one to the other without my being told of it. The old man said to me:'He whom you see behind me was in front of me,' and he explained, 'It is I who am the Chief, to-day as the other time, and in front of this man, as behind him. But two years ago we did not know you, and he showed himself in my place.' It is not unusual to fail to recognize the real chief right away, but it makes one stop and think. And I propose to analyse the machinery of our administration through the chiefs, bearing this incident in mind.

In all territorial administration the native chiefs act as cogwheels between the colonial authority and the native peoples. In French West Africa, which is a federation of colonies, the supreme authority in each colony is vested in the Governor. Within the colony, authority is exercised, in the name of the Governor and under his control, by the Commandants of districts (*cercles*); the *cercle* may be divided into subdivisions, but nevertheless it constitutes the administrative unit, and the Commandant of a *cercle* represents the administrative authority. How does the government, which is centred in the *cercle*, establish relations with the native peoples? This is precisely the function of the *cercle*. It is the motor mechanism which directly engages with the native machinery, the canton, which in turn sets in motion a certain number of villages. Colony and *cercle* on the one hand, *cercle*, canton and village on the other, these are the interlocking parts of the administrative machinery. Commandants of *cercles* and heads of

72 FREEDOM AND AUTHORITY IN FRENCH WEST AFRICA

subdivisions belong to the Colonial Administrative Service,[1] and to the Civil Service of the Federation of French West Africa. Chiefs of cantons and villages are the native chiefs properly so-called, and by abbreviation 'the Chiefs'.

In French West Africa, which is eight times the area of France and comprises a population of fifteen millions, the territorial administration is like a power current passing from the 118 *cercles* to the 2,200 cantons and the 48,000 villages. The native policy that affects fifteen million men depends to a considerable degree on the character of the 118 *cercle* Commandants and their collaborators and the 50,000 native chiefs.[2] Native policy is worth what they are worth. It is what their relations with each other and with the native peoples make it.

The importance of these relations must be thoroughly understood. The *Cercle* is only a motor mechanism so long as it is a transformer of energy. The Commandant of the *Cercle* is not truly a commander except in so far as he can understand the chiefs and get a hearing from them. If his authority is to be effective he has to work through the chiefs, in daily contact with them. And this brings me back to what happened to me: authority is like a force running to waste if it contacts a false chief instead of finding the real one. And among the hundred-odd villages of the dozen cantons of my subdivision, I had at least once lost my authority.

What, then, are the characteristics of a real native chief?

As a rule, the chiefs are studied according to the classification used by the administration: first of all the village chief, then the canton chief, sometimes a chief of a province, more rarely still a great chief whom we call king or emperor. But this is merely an account of the hierarchy of authority among the chiefs, and not a definition of the chiefly power itself. But the power of a chief may be defined in relation to its quality rather than its extent; it may happen, for example, that an ordinary village headman wields more power in his village than a chief of a province in his province. Instead of considering chiefs in relation to the hierarchy in which we place them, let us consider their authority as it is exercised in relation to their own territory. And let us remember that the real chief does exist, though he may be concealed.

Chiefs like the one I saw the first time in the village where I learned my lesson are, so to speak, more or less men of straw. They play the

---

[1] In 1937 there were 385 Colonial Administrators in French West Africa, half of them posted to offices at headquarters in each colony.

[2] See the chart on p. 73.

CHIEFTAINSHIPS IN THE COLONIES OF FRENCH WEST AFRICA

	Provincial chiefs, or chiefs of a group of cantons or tribes	Canton chiefs, or chiefs of tribes	Village chiefs or assimilated to that status:				
			Ordinary	Independent	Assimilated (Ward chiefs)	Dependent Divisions	Independent Divisions
SENEGAL	2	135 (auxiliary chiefs, temporary chiefs, chiefs, deputy chiefs)	9,352				
Circonscription of DAKAR and dependencies		1	41		51		
MAURITANIA	3	50	819 village chiefs, or chiefs of divisions or sub-divisions				
GUINEA		262	4,057	8	9 (mixed communes of Konakry and Kankan)		
SOUDAN	1 paramount chief, 8 provincial chiefs or chiefs of a group of tribes	719	10,907	132	15	622	40
NIGER	3	183	6,585	5			
DAHOMEY	5 (known as 'chefs supérieurs)	161	3,494		20		
IVORY COAST	10	516 canton chiefs, 62 tribal chiefs, 117 chiefs of groups of tribes	11,892				
Totals	52	2,206	47,147	145	95	622	40
					48,049		

74 FREEDOM AND AUTHORITY IN FRENCH WEST AFRICA

part which, in certain big department stores, is assigned to the employé who has to receive the complaints of short-tempered customers. At any demand from the administration—tax, labour service, recruiting, census, new crops to be tried—the fake chief is put forward. On him will fall the wrath of a hoodwinked administration. The reason for this is that the Administration bothers the chiefs too much; it harasses them by perpetually summoning them for meetings; it hustles them with constant demands, exhausts them with requisitions, holds them responsible, on pain of forfeiting their property or even their liberty, for the carrying out of all the orders which it pours out at random. Is it any wonder that the chiefs take refuge in tricks and stratagems? Or else it disconcerts them by issuing directives which it has not succeeded in making plain to them; which means that it is a bad transformer of energy. The inadequacy or the faults of an administration may be measured by the number of 'straw chiefs' which come between it and the real chiefs.

There are other reasons also, which go deep into the heart of African affairs. There are cases where custom decrees that relations with strangers outside the tribe should be regulated by special functionaries, lower in rank than the chief. Thus traders, whether travelling or resident, are the concern of a special minister known as Chief of the market or Chief of strangers. In some parts of Africa, colonials are regarded in the same way as the merchants in the market, strangers who pitch their camp to-day and are gone to-morrow. This in itself shows that only material transactions can be carried out with them.

In the social function of the true chief, at the core of his authority, is a spiritual quality which a stranger cannot apprehend and may not touch. The very life of the country is dependent on the chief. If the Administration fails to understand him, that life withdraws itself; if he is humiliated, it is wounded; if he is overthrown, it is extinguished. To let the chief be seen is rashly and immodestly to expose that holy part where the body social can be mortally wounded.

Canton chiefs rarely have 'straw chiefs'. Obviously it is more difficult for them than for village chiefs to hide themselves and mislead the Administration. But, more than this, it seems that after fifty years of colonization, the spiritual quality of native power has left the big chiefs to take refuge with the small ones, who have not been so much affected by European influence.

It is often said that the colonial administration was wrong in breaking the power of African potentates, and that it is now necessary

THE NATIVE CHIEFS 75

to restore their traditional authority. But where were these great chiefs? With a few exceptions—such as the Mogho-Naba of Ouagadougou among the Mossi—the countries that were conquered at the end of the last century had lost their sovereigns during the slave-trading epoch. And many of the natural chiefs had been more or less detached from their traditional functions through the influence of Moslem proselytizing, long before the French colonial era.

Certainly some of the appointments made were open to criticism: cases where the chiefdom was created at the same time as the chief, or where a man was appointed to a chiefdom to which he had no right. Thus some of the chiefs appointed were the personal employés of the Administration, or even slaves, while the old families of the country were passed over. Here again the villages, which seemed unimportant, were left undisturbed and it was mainly chiefs of cantons whom we appointed. These things, in fact, did not encroach on custom as much as has been supposed. For most of the great chiefs who were displaced by our nominees were themselves feudatories who held their fiefs from the slave-trader for whom they rounded up the game, or they were the soldiers of a Moslem war lord who handed over the pagan cultivators to them as serfs. They did not express, they rather oppressed the old Africa of the land and the villages. And in replacing them by our chiefs of cantons, we have most often merely substituted for a usurper a sort of functionary.

The canton is in most cases a former feudal province turned into an administrative district. *The village, on the other hand, is not an administrative creation. It is still a living entity.* And, in spite of appearances, it is the *village* chief who retains the ancient, intrinsically African authority.

In former times, the chieftainship everywhere had the same simplicity of structure as in the village, whether it concerned a province or the suzerainty over an aggregate of provinces. The words 'kingdom' or 'empire' give an inaccurate idea of it. If we examine the derivation of the generic names of the big chiefs who still exist—the Amenokhall of the Tuareg; the Ardo, the Rouga or the Mani of the Fulani; the Mogho-Naba of the Mossi; the Damel of the Wolof; and many others whose names ring in the chronicles of the earliest travellers, we find an original philological flowering. Our appellation, 'great chief', is as summary and superficial in negro Africa as it would be in Europe to-day, where the Germanic Fuhrer was not the Latin Duce.

The great African chiefdoms were, in their essential character, identical with the smallest ones. Empires and kingdoms had the same

76 FREEDOM AND AUTHORITY IN FRENCH WEST AFRICA

political organization and were of the same social essence as the village. The Soudanese Empire of Soundiata Keita issued from the village of Kangaba and spread over all the regions of the Soudan, to shrink back later to the village that gave it birth. While it lasted it raised a gigantic pyramid which reproduced at the apex the same arrangement as at the base. Or rather it was the village of Kangaba itself stretched out to an empire. Just as in our own day the habitation of the biggest chief only differs from that of his humblest subject by the number of huts put side by side—the same huts for everyone—so the structure of an empire was only made up of a collection of villages. He who knows the village knows the eternal Africa.

We are incapable of such simplicity. There is no differentiation of powers—the chief possesses them all. At one and the same time, and generation after generation, he has been leader of the army, judge, political sovereign and master of home affairs. We think he mixes everything together; we cannot get used to the idea that he *is* everything together. If he delegates his powers he does so *en bloc* and often to a slave. We notice that he has Ministers around him, but they seem to be dignitaries with no clearly regulated functions: the chief of the horsemen, for instance, does not concern himself only with the cavalry—he also has strange religious prerogatives.

We speak of restoring the traditional authority of these sovereigns of the past, without understanding that by introducing our notion of differentiation of powers we have in fact shaken the community more profoundly than if we had shown lack of consideration for its chief. Of what use is it to respect a symbol if we empty it of its meaning?

The chieftainship had a unity derived from the solidarity of the community. The chief led the same kind of life as his people. An Emir of the Moors to-day, who lives in a house in St. Louis-in-Senegal, who gets into his car to go and visit the tribe, is no longer a chief in the native sense of the word. He may well be a progressive man, but in fact he leaves the people without a chief. It is not from a house that he can govern tents; it is not in a car that he can be understood by a community of camel drivers.

The secret of this simplicity, unity, solidarity, is still to be found in the village. It is that the chief's power is the religious bond which unites all the members of the community. *This is a much older religion than Islam*, and it comes from the earth rather than from heaven. It is the communion of a human group with the earth to which it prays in order to cultivate it. The chief is the descendant of the first cultivators of the land. He perpetuates that family and distributes to the

THE NATIVE CHIEFS

living the fields of the earliest dead; in the name of the original family, he hands on the knowledge he has received—knowledge of the soil and of the animals, some of them hostile, some protectors. In 1923, in the Maradi subdivision in the Niger Territory, where there reigned a sultan, the administrator wanted a piece of land for an agricultural research station, and applied to the sultan, the only chief he knew. The sultan was a fine aristocratic figure, with curled locks, clad in a handsome embroidered robe and foaming turban, shod with boots of stamped leather, wearing his sword on his hip, and riding a stallion hung with leather and lengths of cotton cloth, followed by trumpet-blowers and a numerous retinue; he left his vaulted and terraced castle and led the Commandant to the outskirts of the town. A man was summoned to meet them there who was quite unknown to the administrator, a person without prestige or arms. He was the descendant of the original family, the earliest occupants of the soil. He was the master of the land, he alone had the power to lend a piece of it.[1]

In Hausa country, the canton chief is the *Serky*, the landlord. The Sultan of Maradi is called the *Serky n'Fulani*. Now the generic name of the village is *Gari*, but the village chief is not called *Serky n'Gari*, but *Mai-Gari*. A cameleer is the *Mai-rakumi*, a horseman is the *Mai-doki*, that is, 'the camel-man', 'the horse-man'. Thus it appears that the *Mai-Gari* is not the lord of the village, but the village-man, one with the village as the cameleer is one with his camel, and the horse-man one with his horse. I give the idea for what it is worth. I am trying to express the fact that among all the men of the village, the chief is the one who symbolizes the village itself. And I am trying to mark the difference in kind between the *Serky*, the seignior, who may hold numerous villages, and the *Mai-Gari*, who is not a chief of an inferior grade, a bottom-of-the-ladder chief, but in fact the real chief of ancient rural Africa.

A passage from Ernest Renan's *Souvenirs d'Enfance et de Jeunesse*, throws light on the character of the true chief. Speaking of the old Breton chiefs, in connection with the 'flax-bruiser's daughter', he writes that they were 'keystones in the social structure of the people'. The comparison holds good for negro Africa. If you succeed in building your administration round the chief, the whole population will be included. And if he goes with you, they will follow.

---

[1] 'The inalienability of land rights is so rooted in the mind of the African, that in his eyes even the conquest of a region cannot entail any rights whatsoever over the soil conquered.' (Capt. N'Tchoréré, of the Colonial Infantry, 'Le Problème des jeunes générations africaines' in the *Revue des Troupes coloniales*, Dec. 1938.)

78 FREEDOM AND AUTHORITY IN FRENCH WEST AFRICA

It does not matter if the chief is old, infirm or blind; the essential thing is that he should be there.[1] If necessary he can take a young and active man as his colleague. If he is illiterate and has some difficulty in dealing with natives educated in our schools, let him be given clerks and assistants. Only one thing counts, and it does not depend on education, age or health: that is the sacred character of his power. In the old Africa the community which the chief represents lives in him and there can be no life without a supernatural element. Hence the force which binds the people to the chief; hence the ritual which permeates social unity and solidarity, which orders the form of greeting addressed by the people to the chief and gives a religious sanction to the authority of the humblest village chief, the chief of the cultivated and inhabited land.

What principles of action in colonial administration can be drawn from these facts? We must proceed, so to speak, from the 'straw chief' to the chief of the land, who seems indeed to be the product of the land itself, and it is almost always in the village that he is to be found. Thus we are driven to make an important distinction between the village chief and the chief of a canton.

THE CHIEF OF A CANTON: A FEUDAL RULER WHO DISCHARGES THE DUTIES OF AN OFFICIAL

As the village chief derives from a primitive feudal Africa based on the holding of land, so the chief of a canton belongs to modern Africa, and is part of the mechanism of colonial administration.

First, let us put a question of tactics. We often ask ourselves whether the territorial Command should be concentrated in a single station, or whether it should be deployed in a network of small stations grouped about the principal one. Should there be a *cercle* without subdivisions, or a *cercle* composed of subdivisions? The solution of this problem varies according to the number and importance of the canton chiefs.

Take as a starting point the following fact of experience: *The presence of a European administrative organization beside a canton chief tends to limit his independence while at the same time extending his influence.* The chief who lives in the neighbourhood of our offices

---

[1] The best administrative instructions relating to chiefs and to territorial administration are those issued by Gov. general J. van Vollenhoven (*Une âme de Chef*, Plon, 1920) and Gov. general J. Brévié (*La Politique et l'administration indigènes en A.O.F.*, 1931–5. Govt. Printer, Gorée). These were followed, from 1940–1 by the Directives of Gov. general Felix Eboué.

THE NATIVE CHIEFS 79

adapts himself to their surveillance and profits from their activity. And if he becomes less free than other chiefs farther away, he nevertheless acquires pre-eminence over them. He can easily get in touch with the Commandant; he performs services for the colonials; he is introduced to the ways of the administration; he seems doubly chief because he is chief at headquarters.

In a district formed of a homogeneous country, of one race and religion, where the outstanding figure is a feudal grandee who has been appointed chief of a canton or several cantons, there is every advantage in establishing and concentrating the administration in the neighbourhood of the chief, and not constituting subdivisions. If, however, the chief's power seems troublesome or dangerous, the partition of the territory into different *cercles* or into subdivisions will certainly break it up. But it must be realized that then new chiefs will spring up round each subdivision headquarters, and that by lopping branches off the big tree one does not always clear a space for the people, but may only make room for feudal shoots to spring up.

In a district composed of different countries where a number of independent chiefs exist, it will be wise to create several subdivisions and put the headquarters of each in the canton that is most important from the economic point of view. If the differences between the countries are very marked, it may be better to establish a single district and a centralized command.

Is it expedient to lay down rules for all these possible circumstances? It could be argued that a multiplicity of small chiefs of different cantons calls for the same tactics of concentrated command as the existence of a single great chief. The only axiom that will guide us in every case is that the political value of a canton chief is tied up with the economic value of his chiefdom. We need not hesitate to move the headquarters of *cercles* or subdivisions according to the economic progress of the cantons. No native feudal tradition can stand against a railway station, a factory, a market.

If we consider the chiefs in relation to their functions and modes of appointment, we shall recognize other differences between the village chief and the chief of a canton, and shall grasp the fact that the canton chief has become an official.

The administration nominates all chiefs, whoever they may be and in all circumstances. The most frequent case is also the simplest; the Government has only to follow native custom, which varies from hereditary succession to election, according to the locality. Certain customs witness to a shrewd political spirit. Here is one that I never

80 FREEDOM AND AUTHORITY IN FRENCH WEST AFRICA

tire of quoting: In the Djerma country, the *Koye*, that is to say the chief, is chosen from the family of the ancestor who ruled the Djermas when they occupied the country many centuries ago. But he is chosen by a council, called the council of 'Zendis', composed of the principal descendants of the original inhabitants. The Djermas are the invaders; the Zendis, the invaded. By calling the sons of the vanquished to choose from among the victors the chief over all, the unknown African sage who founded this custom invites us to follow it. Which is what we do. And the Djerma *Koye* of Dosso is at present one of the greatest chiefs of the Federation.

Greater care is needed where there is no hereditary dynasty or well-established rule to take into account. There are two cases to be considered: either the chief will be drawn from the country, or from outside. Except in very rare cases the village chief will never come from outside. If the family which provided the village head has died out, it is still from within the area that the branch must be chosen which will bear the new chief. And if the whole village is awakening to a new life, it will be possible to arrange for an election on a broad basis including not only notables and heads of families, but also the young people and women.

It is, however, in the exercise of his functions rather than by the method of his appointment that the chief of a canton differs from a village chief and acts as an agent of the Administration.

The primary function of a chief, whether he is chief of canton or village, is to be there, to be in residence. Nothing takes the place of the real presence. If the courtyard of a *cercle* Commandant is always paved with chiefs waiting for him to receive them, we can be sure that the administration is not good. The Commandant who keeps his chiefs at headquarters, far from their chiefdoms, injures their authority and his own. And indirectly he oppresses the villages. In fact, in order to put in an appearance at headquarters, the chiefs drain their territories, where they are represented by deputies who oppress the peasants. There is another method, which consists in requiring the canton chiefs to maintain representatives at headquarters. This procedure may be a bad one if these representatives are themselves a heavy charge, and if they encroach on the status of the chiefs.

In fact, we are confronted with opposing and mutually contradictory necessities: on the one hand we are well aware that it is essential to preserve the native character of the canton chief and to make use of the traditional feudal spirit which still survives in him; on the other hand the very fact of colonization forces us to shape him to our ad-

THE NATIVE CHIEFS 81

ministrative outlook. Our major fault is lack of method in our dealings with him. We demand from him too many trivial tasks and we
set too much store by the way in which he performs them. Instead of
entrusting to him certain important tasks—a tax, a main road, a new
crop—and judging his achievement on the spot in our tours, we make
his authority a travesty by using him as an intermediary in small
affairs—provisioning a camp, receiving a vaccinator, collecting witnesses. for a petty court case, providing a supply of chickens. We
think that because he is a native, we are carrying out a native policy
with his assistance, while in fact by putting menial tasks on him we
treat him as sub-European. And we tolerate a hypocritical manœuvre:
in theory, the canton chief executes administrative orders; in practice, he resorts to feudal methods to get them carried out. He turns
the tax into feudal tribute, the labour service into a *corvée* and cultivation into requisitioning.

Should the traditional authority of the canton chief be restored?
We have already shown that this is a negative programme. We could
certainly reconstitute a décor of pomp and ceremony around them,
but we should not be able to re-create the soul of their ancient authority. No, the tendency of the Administration is all towards making
these feudalists into officials. But then we must face the thing. They
should be specialized officials and exercise a distinctive function. We
have already involved them in implicit officialdom; they receive
rebates on the tax, which is not always without danger for the taxpayers; they are paid a salary and it is small enough; on the Ivory
Coast there are 500 of them to share 1,500,000 francs, while the European administration of the *Cercles* costs 7,430,000. They enjoy a status
of a sort, in the sense that they do not come under the 'Native Status
Code',[1] and that they cannot be arbitrarily deposed. They have a
personal file in the records at the station and they are scrupulously
given good and bad marks by their Commandants. They are decor-
ated, they are welcomed at receptions on national holidays, they are
invited to visit exhibitions; they are sent as delegates to Dakar and
even to Paris; they are brought together on councils where they
collaborate with Europeans. And they are rightly treated as important
persons; but what is needed is not to re-establish them, but to establish them. Not to re-establish them in a social structure that is dying,
but to establish them in a modern Africa that is being born. And it is

[1] Translator's note: This 'Indigenat' is a disciplinary code, applied by administrative officials to all persons legally of native status, i.e. not French citizens, nor
of any legally defined intermediate status.

82 FREEDOM AND AUTHORITY IN FRENCH WEST AFRICA

there that we should make officials of them. This need not mean making them robots or abstractions. To make officials of them is first to define their official duties, and then to establish not only their administrative status but their social personality. We must reconsider with them—and for them, as for ourselves—the problem of the function of the chief.

The Village Chief: Let the Village re-create its own Chief

For a long time to come, the territorial Administration will work through canton chiefs who, while no longer feudal, are not yet completely officials. But there is a basic Africa on which *cercles* and cantons will always rest: the Africa of the villages. It is in the village that the secret of African evolution is hidden. Do not let us be afraid to sweep Africa clean of its feudalists by officializing them, and to dig right down to the rock, to the foundations of ancient negro society. Here are rooted the local institutions which influence native policy and transform the conditions of territorial Administration. The councils of village notables have had a status in the administration for several years; they deliberate in each *cercle* on the plan of campaign for labour service and on the tax-rate. In the villages themselves these councils should not be the preserve of the notables, but should include all the heads of families. It is also necessary to revive and adapt to modern Africa a very old institution, the association of young people of the same age, which embodies the principles, the disciplines and the chartered liberties of a trade union. The councils and age associations will not take the place of the village chief, but they will help to bring him to life in a new form.

The feudal organization that we found in Africa is crumbling. And the village that supported it, and which we did not discover at first, is going to pieces. With our commercial economy, we have introduced an individualistic ferment which has now reached the village and is eating away the ancient community. The canton chief is losing his feudal character and the village chief his religious sanctions. But though it is conceivable that the canton chief may become an official, it is difficult to foresee what the village chief will become. It is not the case that there are great chiefs who could be chiefs of cantons, and small chiefs who could be village chiefs. There is one feudal Africa which may be compared to the feudal structure of French society at the close of the Middle Ages. Just as the French kings gathered into

THE NATIVE CHIEFS

one unity the land of France, so in Africa the Colonial Government unites the country by eliminating the great territorial overlords and changing the feudatories into chiefs of cantons or officials. A colonial Africa is developing, overlapping the rural Africa of the village chiefs, who themselves are also feudatories and whose importance—legal and social—is not to be measured by the size of their territories. The area which they rule is not large but it represents the land which was reclaimed from the bush by the first cultivators, whose lineage it perpetuates. The village chiefs have preserved the genius of the land and of labour. But to-day their position is shaken by new methods of labour and new forms of tenure. What new kind of man will arise as chief in this Africa? I do not think that he will be an official. He will emerge from the families who hold the land and from the world of labour. But in what form who can yet say?

A curious fact seems to me pregnant with meaning for the future. Good year or bad, there are 50,000 to 70,000 migrant groundnut labourers—*Navetanes*—who go off from the Soudan to Senegal, and 100,000 cocoa *Navetanes* who go from the Upper Volta to the Ivory Coast and the Gold Coast—a seasonal migration of agricultural labourers. These peasant labourers have chiefs, not the chiefs of their own original villages nor yet those of the villages in the south where they go to work. The village of their birth may be a thousand miles from the place where they work, and it will be a year before they are back there. The village where they work is foreign in race and customs. And yet the *Navetanes* have their chief. The Administration had no hand in it, they found him themselves. Men from the same Soudanese village or region have drawn from among themselves the chief of the work-team; he organizes their movements, buys the railway tickets or fixes the stages on the road, settles the team in at the place of work and oversees it. Thus rural labour, in this new form of seasonal migrants, can have new chiefs. And in the agrarian Africa of our time, there may be a work-chief distinct from the territorial chief. The capacity of Africa to produce new chiefs is not bound to the traditional form of the territorial administration.

What is certain is that the village will always have to have a chief. That is of moment not only to the colonial administration but to Africa itself. There will be a chief, that is to say there will be only one. In every country in the world, the ruler is a single individual. The old Africa, with its own forces of renewal, will perhaps construct a 'municipium', a communal organization, but in it it will place the chief.

84 FREEDOM AND AUTHORITY IN FRENCH WEST AFRICA

Do not let us be too closely mixed up in it. We can constitute the canton; we should leave the village to react and reconstitute itself. The *de facto* chief that the village gives birth to will be the legal chief in our eyes.

VI. LAW AND CUSTOM

IN French West Africa there are magistrates who administer justice according to the French legal Code, and others who administer local Customary law; and those who come under their jurisdiction, like the magistrates themselves, are divided into two different classes. The Code applies to French citizens, whatever their colour; Customary law applies to native subjects whatever their rank. And it is laid down that customary law is applicable in so far as it is not contrary to the principles of civilization.[1]

Since the subject of this study is territorial administration it might seem that we should confine ourselves to Customary law. The administration of native customary law is a branch of native policy and of territorial administration. The tribunal is an observation post from which the administrative officer who presides over it may study the effects of his own administration and the reactions of the people he governs. The African world is revealed to him. Litigants in civil cases and those accused of crimes will make plain to him the character of the customs and social habits of the country. And in pronouncing judgment he effects political actions; he maintains civil peace as well as public order; he recognizes and observes native rights, and by pursuing justice he stimulates their evolution.

Why then discuss the Code? Customary law is all that needs to be considered. I believe that it is no longer possible to separate Custom from the Code. The Code dominates native law more or less explicitly and, strangely enough, native law is beginning to infiltrate into the Code. In the administration of native law, in this very important aspect of native policy, Code and Custom are in contact and in conflict.

The Code: Its Jurisdiction in Criminal Matters

First we shall discuss the theory that the Code should oust the customary law and be made applicable to natives. It is alleged that

---

[1] This was written in 1939. The decree of April 1946 abolished native penal law and placed all the inhabitants of French Negro Africa under the jurisdiction of the French Code and French penal laws.

86 FREEDOM AND AUTHORITY IN FRENCH WEST AFRICA

the Code has great advantages. Handled with a sure touch by professional judges it is a precise instrument of justice. It shines by comparison with the vague and fluid character of customary law. Moreover, professional magistrates are clearly superior to the judges in native courts, who may be enlightened administrators or shrewd native elders but, for all that, have no solid legal training. The Code is so exact in its application and so well directed by its own past history that the judgments which it produces are inevitably just and constitute in themselves a cultural value.

Nevertheless, some objections come to mind. Doesn't the Code sometimes trouble the natives' sense of equity? Do the natives understand something which the magistrates of the Code freely admit, the *vice de forme*—dismissal of a case because the charge has been incorrectly drawn? And not to speak of faulty drafting, do the natives really distinguish between several counts? An African lorry-driver has been convicted eleven times for infringement of traffic rules; he is sentenced on the twelfth occasion to a few days' imprisonment for the same offence, in committing which he caused an accident involving injury to several persons in the lorry he was driving. The sentence is quashed because he was only charged with one delict, though he had committed two distinct misdemeanours, one that of contravening a police regulation, the other of having injured his passengers; pending his trial, according to the rules, he is liberated, and he himself cannot make head or tail of the whole affair.

Another thing. To speak of a Code obviously implies sanctions. But our Code applies some sanctions that have a strange impact on the natives. For example, the Code has no knowledge of corporal punishment and torture, apart from the death penalty, and it does not in general impose other penalties than prison. Now imprisonment is not always understood in the same way among the peoples of French West Africa. In one place it seems an adventure that has nothing dishonourable about it; in another, on the contrary, it is equivalent to being condemned to death. There are some Africans who, if you put them in prison, will become a sort of domestic servant, and end by regarding themselves as members of your family. But if you imprison a Fulani he will die.

And again, is the Code comprehensive enough for the natives? Does it really provide for everything we should consider criminal that may be committed in Africa? Open the French Code and look for the crime of cannibalism there. If a man who died a natural death is eaten before he is buried, and this macabre meal has not been the occasion of a sale, where is the crime under the Code? There has been no assassination, no violation of burial, no illicit commerce. There is only a ritual banquet partaken of by pious kinsfolk, who have respected native custom without infringing the Code. And does the Code provide for acts which are regarded as crimes in Africa itself? Open the Code and look for the crime of witchcraft. In 1926, in the Mossi country, a man died of an illness, and public rumour accused an old sorceress of having killed him. Poison was suggested, an autopsy was carried out—nothing was revealed. The rumour persists and a disturbance of public order is threatened if the person regarded as guilty is not arrested and punished. The sorceress, when interrogated, far from denying, confesses; she asserts that she killed at a distance, by casting a spell. When a village wants to stone a person accused of a crime that we do not admit the possibility of, when the accused herself asserts that she has committed a crime which to our minds cannot be committed, what do you do with your Code?

When, under the French Code, you judge a native accused of a crime, you summon a court of assizes, and in so doing you summon a jury. And, in the French West Africa of our day, the jury contains a majority of Europeans, more susceptible to emotion than professional magistrates, less informed about native psychology than administrators who judge according to praetorian law. In practice, will not these Europeans allow themselves to be carried away by racial feeling? This fear is so well-founded that in the Belgian Congo the institution of the jury does not exist. And, the Code being the same for all, if some day the majority of the jury is composed of black citizens, will not a white person suffer prejudice?

The application of the Code to natives is not a simple matter, and some even of those who advocate the use of the Code have said: Let us apply the Code in criminal cases and leave civil cases to the jurisdiction of native law. In fact, in spite of all the objections that may be put forward, the Code must prevail over Custom in criminal cases. This is an act of sovereignty and, as such, Africans will readily accept it. They know that justice is one of the outstanding attributes of the chief, and we should abuse our power in their eyes if we deprived it of our law. But more than this, it is the recognition of an actual state of affairs in native society; for, as soon as the question of penal sanctions arises, Custom becomes a fiction. In the course of fifty years of colonization the penal sanctions of customary law have ceased to be operative. It is laid down that corporal punishment and torture shall always be replaced by fines or imprisonment. What sort of

88 FREEDOM AND AUTHORITY IN FRENCH WEST AFRICA

African Custom is it when its penalties are Europeanized? And that is not all. Custom has in fact lost its spiritual validity. By abolishing trial by ordeal; by restricting swearing on the Koran or fetishes; by not taking into account the supernatural elements attaching to the person of the judge; by stripping the chiefs of their judicial power and appointing as assessors at tribunals men who are no longer the inspired initiates of the old days; by doing all this, have we not emptied custom of its substance? What indeed is a religious tradition which has been secularized? Finally, it is laid down that we are to apply native law in so far as it does not run counter to the principles of our civilization. But what are these principles, if not those of the Code? Where else are they defined than in the Code? When we say that we judge according to custom, we really mean that we begin by judging customary law itself according to the Code. In fact, in penal matters custom is dead. Let us bury it, and allow the Code to live in an amended form, adapted to Africa and supplemented by a special penal code.

A Code is necessary to supersede the judgments of the native law which by their inconsistency betray their arbitrary nature. On 18 March 1927, a village headman, charged with failing to inform the authorities of the escape of a prisoner, was acquitted. Eight days earlier, the same tribunal had convicted a man of the same village for not having reported the discovery of human bones. A certain tribunal, on one day in May 1934, heard two cases of unintentional homicide; the same magistrates on the same day found one a crime and the other a delict. There must be an end to the uncertainty about what acts are to be regarded as crimes. Africans have a right to consistent justice and it is not to be found in the native customary law, which varies in different places and with different judges; which is nowhere recorded or interpreted by any jurisprudence worth the name. They have a right to the Code.

CUSTOMARY LAW; ITS POWER IN CIVIL MATTERS
THE JURIDICAL VALIDITY OF THE VILLAGES

So much for criminal matters. As for civil cases, here the defenders of customary law have a better case. They point out that the application of the Code, instead of establishing order, makes trouble, and even hinders the progress of the natives. Africans, they tell us, are so firmly attached to their customs that zealous judges often revise our official judgments, which are based on a wrong interpretation of customary law. And because customary law is not understood by our tribunals a great number of cases do not come before them.

We do not understand the customary law because we do not trust it and our knowledge of it is only superficial. We try to do things too well, and on the pretext that native courts are guilty of abuses and native judges not above bribery, and that customary judgments are often very curious, we shrink from entrusting judicial functions to natives and allowing free play to the local customary law.

We do not hesitate to appoint an African magistrate to administer our own law, but we are reluctant to invest a native with authority under his own customary law. We prefer to create artificial judiciaries which are native only in name. The Belgians and the British, on the other hand, recognize the native tribunals and rightly find in them the germs of native administration; being strictly practical they consider that the absence of native law is a greater danger than the errors of the magistrates.

We are fundamentally ignorant about customary law. The defects and the barbarisms which we attribute to it derive from our ignorance of its true nature. We do not rightly understand it, because we only know it through an interpreter. We do not perceive its juridical value because we have not grasped the social principles of it. Even those elements which we find most strange have a significance in the social structure of the community though it may escape us. To understand and practise native customary law one needs to be an ethnologist and a sociologist. One cannot administer justice by transplanting European regulations on to African soil, but only by studying those who are amenable to it. Customary law cannot be studied from written records, because no such records were kept in the past; nor is it simply one aspect of African culture; a true understanding of native custom comes from a certain attitude to life in Africa and the identification of oneself with the people.

Custom is an intrinsically African reality, absolutely incapable of being reduced to terms of our law. Africans do not distinguish between Criminal Law and Civil Law, and they have no categories of Civil Law. As regards Criminal Law, we have agreed to apply the Code. But Criminal Law should not usurp too much of the field. Leave the natives their civil custom. It is the breath of their social life, and as it stands it deals with matters of commerce, matrimony, and land tenure, without dividing them into clear-cut categories. But as it stands, it is a living whole. If you submitted it to the influence of your Code, if you cut it up into categories, you would kill native

90   FREEDOM AND AUTHORITY IN FRENCH WEST AFRICA

society. You would build an elegant framework of abstractions within which the cases you judge would become merely cases, and no longer living persons. You would put a premium on detribalization; you would be favouring the minority, which has abandoned the community and become absorbed in the towns. You would penalize the masses who themselves are progressing, but not in the same way as those whom we call 'progressive'. Instead of treating custom as an old house with unsafe foundations and not worth repairing, let it live and it will evolve; the younger generation will see to that.[1]

In Christian villages, for example, customs will arise which will have vitality and value; this may perhaps be the starting-point for an improvement in the condition of women. You may trust the younger generation to see that custom does not stagnate. Questions of the age of marriage and of fraudulent marriage could well be settled by customary law, and probably more efficiently than by the Code.

There are Africans now who are educated, not simply to imitate us but to use our modes of thought to express themselves. Give them a share in the administration of customary law. They will react against the polygamous practices of old men who monopolize the young girls. They will initiate the custom of fixing the age for marriage so that the consent of the girl is obtained. They will influence local custom in the direction of monogamy—a practice which is already becoming habitual among them.

As the territories of French West Africa, being federated, tend to develop a common way of life, so local customs in different areas tend to influence and approximate to each other. Learn from the people themselves, not only the customs of the past, but those of the present day, and you will probably discover permanent qualities and general characteristics which will enable you to see the African, not as someone strictly limited by his own narrow environment of savanna or forest, and subjugated by his ancestors, but as a free personality in a new Africa.

But take care! Do not hasten to codify these permanent qualities and general characteristics. Collect them by all means but let them keep their status of customs. Be conscious of the quality of customary law; it has indeed been mutilated, since in criminal matters it is becoming increasingly dominated by the spirit of the Code, and it might be supposed that in consequence of being restricted to civil

---

[1] In this direction a very interesting move has recently been made by the Administration. See Gov.-Gen. Brévié's directives (the first dated 19 March 1931) and the study published by Bernard Maupoil, *Coutumiers juridiques de l'A.O.F.* Larose, 1939.

cases it would gradually disappear. But in fact it issues from such profound depths of African life that it continues to grow and even to influence the Code. Here is an example drawn from the actual legal position in native communities. For a long time African customary law was not legally recognized since the situations to which it applied did not fall within any of the categories provided for by French law. Supposing a chief tried to establish in the courts, in accordance with the Code, the traditional rights exercised by a village over its own land. According to the customary law, the administrator, acting as judge and assisted by native assessors, would recognize such rights; he recognized the legal status of the village and its capacity to own, and assert its rights of ownership over, the land on which it was built and which it cultivated. But when the matter passed out of the jurisdiction of Custom and into that of Law, and the chief appeared, not before the tribunal of the administrative officer, but before the court of the professional magistrate, difficulties arose. The customary rights of the village were not questioned, but their exercise was found to be invalid. The magistrate enquired in what capacity the chief appeared. As representing the village—true, but what, according to the Code, is the legal status of the group known as a village? Is it a public utility company, a society, an association, a syndicate, a corporate body, an association of owners? The magistrate searched through the Code and found nothing. The African village exists in fact but has no means of proving its existence in law. It exists within the framework of customary law, but has no power to act within the framework of French law. See what serious consequences flow from this situation, in which the land rights of the native population are in danger of being abolished and the villages of being juridically annihilated.

Now on 3 November 1934 the Court of Appeal at Dakar, the supreme court of French West Africa, for the first time took cognizance of the nature of customary law in its own legal practice. Custom was not made definitely subordinate to the Code, nor was its value assessed on the basis of its capacity to produce results acceptable to the Code. The fundamental principles of customary law were examined and the consequences necessarily resulting from those principles were determined. The court decided two questions: first—what was the legal basis of the African village? The court's decision was that the French legislature, by proclaiming its recognition of local custom, placed the village on a legal basis entirely distinct from anything provided for in French law and did not require the African village to be amenable to French municipal regulations.

92   FREEDOM AND AUTHORITY IN FRENCH WEST AFRICA

In order to recognize the legal status of the village and of the land rights which it asserts, the court must define custom and legislate in accordance with it. The second question was, who is qualified to represent the village in law? The court found that the village chief, pleading in his own name as a member of the village community, in defence of the rights which he personally enjoyed as a member of that community, established by that action the legal status of the community and the validity of its rights.

This decree of 3 November 1934 deserves study. It establishes the legal status of village chiefs, and it marks a new orientation of French law in Africa, pointing the way to a solution of the conflict between Code and Custom by means of a development of French law.

VII. THE SPHERE OF THE DIVINE

THE authority of the African Chief has a sacred character; no doubt this will disappear, but at present it exists and must be taken into account. When an administrative officer in the course of his duties enters into relations with the chief of a district or a village, causing him to execute orders or to take action, the administrator, a secular official, enters the sphere of the divine. And this does not apply only to chiefs. At every contact, even to-day, with native life he meets the impact of religion. In the political reactions of the people, in their habits of work and their modes of life, religion is always an invisible factor. Problems which to all appearance concern only agricultural production, conceal a religious element. It is no paradox to say that the most useful of all animals to native agriculture in Africa is the chicken, the animal which the peasant offers in sacrifice with prayer before choosing his plot of land, before clearing it, imploring rain for it, cultivating it and gathering in the harvest.

Finally, the native religions, as one is tempted to call them, are not the only ones in action. The Colonial Administration has to recognize the importance and follow the development of those which it has, so to speak, imported. It is no longer Islam and fetishism so much as Christianity which is creating new social conditions in Africa and is modifying administrative practice. Moreover, the Administration is becoming increasingly an arbiter on the temporal plane between different religions. To sustain this rôle, a sympathetic understanding of religious sentiment and a well-defined idea of what constitutes the secular sphere are needed.

CHRISTIANITY AND NATIVE POLICY

To return to the distinction we have drawn between 'colony' and native territory: on the colonial side we have Christianity—not only the Christian religion but all that Christian civilization has bestowed on the colony.

94 FREEDOM AND AUTHORITY IN FRENCH WEST AFRICA

At the beginning of the modern colonial era it was quite simple: religion and civilization were inextricably mingled within the context of Christianity. Europe was Christendom. It never imagined that the discovery of the West Indies (America) might give birth to any state that was not Christian. Pope Alexander Borgia, in 1494, at the end of the Middle Ages, divided the world outside Europe into two parts, east of the Azores for Portugal, west for Castille. Portuguese and Castilians bound themselves to preach the Faith to the indigenous peoples; the idea never entered their heads that they might not hold to that Faith themselves. They would not have understood that a colony could be founded without the Cross. No conquistadors without chaplains, no caravels without cathedrals. At the dawn of the Renaissance, at the time of the great voyages of discovery and the first movements of colonial expansion, Christianity, in some aspects the heir of the Ancient World, revived the old idea of the religious identity of the mother country and the colony. The Portuguese and Spanish, the French, English and Dutch, did not try to include all the gods in one colonial enterprise, or one imperial practice. For them, the religion of the mother country was the religion of the colony, the basis of colonial law, the link binding together the European kingdom and its oversea provinces. Thus Christianity—Church and State together—advanced into the various new worlds.

But this colonization was shot through with great difficulties. In the colonies as in Europe, Christianity was split between Catholics and Protestants. Some colonies, it is true, were to issue from this very cleavage. On 6 September 1620, the *Mayflower* left Plymouth, carrying to America the Pilgrim Fathers who were quitting Papist England. A century later, there arose in a Puritan England the Methodism of John Wesley, moral source of the pioneer spirit and of British imperial greatness. But Catholic colonies and Protestant colonies do not stand for peace. The livelier their faith, the more tragic the conflict they propagate.

Christianity was to become a prey to yet other upheavals. In Holland, which from the seventeenth century had taken its colonial responsibilities with exemplary seriousness, a French Huguenot traveller, Jean Chardin, produced a scientific humanitarian chronicle,[1] which in some sort anticipated the writings of the 'philosophes' of the eighteenth century. Also in Amsterdam in 1771, was published the Abbé Raynal's *Histoire Philosophique et Politique des Etablissements et du Commerce des Europeans dans les Indes*. The French Revolu-

[1] *Voyage en Perse et aux Indes orientales*, 1683.

THE SPHERE OF THE DIVINE

tion broke out. In 1792 French citizenship was bestowed on the Englishman Wilberforce who preached the abolition of slavery. Article 15 of the Declaration of the Rights of Man and the Citizen, decreed that 'every man may hire his time and his services but no man may sell himself or be sold'. The Revolution was thus at one with Christianity in an essential truth: the dignity of human personality. But nevertheless it appeared as an anti-religious force. It would have reduced religion to a Deistic philosophy. It was not only by destroying slavery that the Revolution had repercussions in the colonies, but also by breaking down family and social traditions and the doctrine of divine right in the old world of the metropolitan countries in Europe; it asserted the right of critical thought, thus carrying on the work of the Reformation; it encouraged individualism; it affected both the Christian religion and Christian civilization. It was the French Revolution even more than the wars of religion which delivered a mortal blow to colonial Christianity.

On the other hand, in the native territories, Christianity came into collision with the idigenous religions. In this collision the defensive reactions of pagan cults constituted a less serious threat than the means of attack with which the colony itself provided them. Engaged in a struggle against the beliefs of the conquered, Christianity was at the same time endangered by the fanatical or pharisaic devotion of the conquerors. While it laboured to convert the natives it was impeded by the sins of the colonials. At a very early date the discord between evangelization and colonization became apparent.

Don Sebastian, King of Portugal, drew up an evangelizing programme for the first colonizers: 'Uproot greed from the hearts of men and cherish those who are crushed down by it.' But almost at once the Spanish Dominican, Bartolomeo de las Casas, the father of the Indians, sorrowfully proclaimed the bitter truth: 'From 1510 at least up to the present year 1564 I do not believe that there has been one man in all the Indies (the Americas) who has not violated or does not violate to-day the most sacred and indisputable principles of honourable dealing.'

A hard materialism always seems to have opposed any spiritual quality in colonial practice. In our own time Werner Sombart the economist writes: 'We have become wealthy because whole populations have died for us; it is for us that continents have been depopulated.' And who are 'we' but the Christians? And Gandhi cried: 'Europe is no longer Christian.'

Out of this situation was evolved Christianity's native policy in the

96 FREEDOM AND AUTHORITY IN FRENCH WEST AFRICA

colonies—the policy of Missions. The Church—and the same is true of the Protestant Churches—does not confine itself to maintaining religion in the 'colony' but labours to evangelize the native territories, and is not afraid to cut itself off from the 'colony' if necessary. The Church relies on the transcendant power of the Christian faith to adapt itself to the most widely differing countries, and adopts a policy of coming to terms with them. Ultimately she establishes a native clergy and sets herself above all colonies, metropolitan countries and empires.

What is this power of adaptation? It does not deny the differences between countries, it rather consecrates and uses them. The Church takes them as they are and seeks to unite them all, without infringing their individualities, in one concord of spiritual life. Far from desiring to rob the natives of their status as persons, she seeks to make that very personality Christian. Nothing can turn her from that path. Contrary to the general opinion, she sets herself to make her cate-chumens proud of being African. In Dahomey, under the influence of the missionaries, urban Africans on Sundays leave off their European clothing and wear their traditional native costume.

The Church goes farther still. She studies native religions and adopts whatever in them she can use. The Church has played a part in rehabilitating Fetishism, which used to be regarded as worthless superstition, but in which has been found a mystical ritual. Just as, in the sixteenth century in the universities of Salamanca where Vitoria taught, the Church acted as an expert in colonial law, and defined the natural law of native peoples, so now she acts as the theologian, so to speak, of Fetishism, in which she recognizes the best means of reaching the soul of the African, and the best founda-tion on which to build with him the new home to which he is being guided.

Missionaries have to speak the native vernacular, which they learn in their training colleges at home; they have to preach in it and teach in it (unless the Administration requires the use of French or English); they compose hymns in it.

But more than this, the missions 'come to terms'—that is, they practise a native policy which eases the transition from paganism to Christianity. From the sixteenth century the Jesuits have practised this method in the Far East (China, Annam and Tonkin). It demands a profound understanding of the native mentality and of human motivation. It captures the country from within, not by external violence.

THE SPHERE OF THE DIVINE

It is impossible to understand the native policy of the Churches—Catholic or Protestant—unless it is realized that, as the logical consequence of their faith, they are international and anti-racialist. Clear evidence of this is provided by the action of the Catholic Church. In his Encyclical of 15 June 1926, addressed to the first six Chinese bishops, Pope Pius XI wrote: 'The work of the missions would be more fruitful if they could destroy the current belief that the activities of the Church and its missionaries subserve the interests and the policies of foreign nations; from which the conclusion is drawn that the Church is hostile to the independence of her converts. Whenever it seems necessary, in order to extend the frontiers of the Church, to transfer missionary activities from one congregation to another, or to entrust new vicariates to native clergy, we shall not hesitate to do so.'

In practice, national conventions are more or less respected, but the international character of the missions is maintained by their methods of recruiting personnel. The African Missions of Lyons, for example, have training colleges in Ireland and in Holland and can appoint Irish or Dutch Fathers to French Africa. The vicariates do not coincide with administrative areas. A vicariate of the White Fathers may include territory in the Ivory Coast and the Gold Coast. But it is primarily in its building up of a native clergy that the Church emphasizes most forcibly the choice it has made.

From the spiritual point of view it could not do otherwise without repudiating the words of St. Paul on which Pius XI, in his letter to the Chinese bishops, comments as follows:

'The name of the Catholic—that is to say universal—Church itself shows that the Church belongs to all nations and includes all peoples, and that by the divine will of Christ its Founder there cannot be within it any distinction of origin or condition; there is no longer Greek or Jew, circumcised or uncircumcised, barbarian or Scythian, bond or free, but Christ is all in all.'

The Protestant churches possess the notion of expiatory exchange, akin to the Catholic doctrine of the Communion of Saints, and they also vigorously assert Christian universalism. Pasteur Lechnardt writes[1] that the whole of colonial practice is included in the rule of human exchange: 'Exchange is a natural law by which all existence is conditioned, and from it, by the exercise of thought, proceed all our notions of contract and law. We must remember that the roots of justice, of sensibility, of social order, lie in the delicate balancing of

[1] No. 59, *Propos missionnaires*, June 1937. Article entitled 'La Colonization'.

98 FREEDOM AND AUTHORITY IN FRENCH WEST AFRICA

these imponderable factors; only thus can one establish with another those exchanges by which individuals and peoples are built up and renewed: thus also may one rediscover the law of colonization.

'In fact no existing system of colonial administration starts from scratch. There is a colonial reality to be dealt with by actual experience: it is the reality of the sinful world. . . . The mission, which is the activity of Christ, is not of this world. But the missionary is a man and himself is a part of the colonial reality. As such he is directly involved in all the evil as well as the good, in all the exchanges which characterize colonization. . . .'

Francis Vernier defined the real greatness of the missionary in the colonies from the point of view of expiation: 'The missionary should not say "I am making reparation for the sins of my fellow countrymen", but "I am expiating our sins". Try as we may we can never disentangle our own thread from the skein of responsibilities involved in colonial enterprises. . . . The faults of any one of my people are my faults and my weakness. . . . Indeed we are all guilty—all of us together.

'By making reparation we do not as it were add an ornament to our individual righteousness, we simply take our right place in the living system of justice—justice in action whose true name is love. . . (But who are we to make reparation for anything? Can we find in our broken lives wherewithal to repair the breaches we have made?) But let us say: "Jesus, make reparation for our faults. I am a cell in the colonial organism, set at one special and particular place which Christ has appointed so that his eternal and atoning life may abide there."

'Neither is there a "colonial" nor a "non-colonial" mission, a mission attached to certain interests, a mission pure and simple or one that is dubious; there is only one work, since there is only one God, one Saviour, one Spirit, one world; one organism with fundamental relationships in which there is traffic in groundnuts, copra, ivory, gold-dust, absinthe and guns, but in which are also found ecstasies of love, spiritual existences, and where the conversion of a Christian citizen in France finds its crown and counterpart in the conversion of a prince on the Zambezi, or of a nameless slave who is now a nobleman of the order of Jesus Christ.

'Companions in the great adventure, servants of Jesus Christ, we dwell in a hidden fastness at the heart of the Universe. May this thought trouble our consciences, open and enlarge our minds, bring to our hearts the peace which is born of communion with the infinite, and to our souls adoration, because the Absolute—by a divine para-

THE SPHERE OF THE DIVINE 99

dox—has entered into history and is summed up in one word—a Name—which may be praised but not spoken.

'The mission works in history, in colonization, and therefore the missionary is the best colonist: his attitude and his life effect the most successful, the most complete, the most life-giving exchanges; he does not yield to the world, or tolerate unjust practices; he brings succour to the suffering world, he elicits and sustains honest effort, so much so that colonists and colonized, whom he worries and helps by turns, soon realize that he himself obeys a Heavenly Father, and through him gain a clearer view of human solidarity and fraternity.'

This native policy of Christianity should be rightly understood. There are African priests trained in the local seminaries of Dahomey and Haute Volta, and there will be African bishops. There are African ministers. But these do not constitute a special order of clergy, confined to natives only, nor are they consecrated by means of a special African form, as certain officers hold a special native rank. The African priest or minister exercises fully all the powers of his office. He has authority over all his congregation whether they are black or white. As priest he hears the confession of the white woman and of the black, he absolves the labourer or the Governor.

Politically the attitude adopted by the Churches has important consequences. They have dissociated themselves from that form of colonial practice which legally recognizes Europeans as the ruling class. Out of the 13,000 priests of Catholic missions throughout the world, 4,400 are natives. In tropical Africa Catholicism is spreading in a pagan environment. Since 1886—the date of the Black Martyrs of Uganda (beatified in 1920)—a huge Catholic stronghold has developed in the region of the Great Lakes, with one and a half million baptized converts (Missions of the White Fathers). Missionary activity in the French Cameroons has had striking results: 26,000 baptisms up to 1914; 170,000 in 1937. The Protestant missions are equally active. In the near future, when the native clergy is well established, we may expect a remarkable increase in the rate of progress of evangelization and an increase also in the crop of political problems it produces.

ISLAM—FETISHISM

Let us now consider religion from the native point of view. What chiefly struck the colonists on their arrival was the incidence of Islam in one area and Fetishism in another; Africa seemed to be divided

100   FREEDOM AND AUTHORITY IN FRENCH WEST AFRICA

between two religions, or rather between a religion—Islam—and a sort of superstition with local variations described as Fetishism. But it soon appeared that throughout Moslem Africa there was a substratum of ancient fetishism, which suggested that Islam in Africa was on the surface rather than a penetration to the depths. At the same time it should be recognized that this Islamization is not merely local—it is very widespread even if it does not go deep. And it is a most serious mistake to limit one's conception of Islam to the persons and the situation within one's own administrative area. In Africa especially there is a Moslem community which was there long before we came, which persists outside the field of our activities and which mocks at our administrative boundaries and our colonial frontiers. Anything which touches a Moslem in one corner of Africa may affect all the Moslems in the world. The administrator should therefore recognize the importance of religious persons without temporal attachments—such as monks and pilgrims. The administrator will find it easier to get on with a layman than with a religious, and he will have less need to keep under observation a powerful theocratic chief, resident in his own area, than a humble wandering pilgrim travelling to Mecca and engaged in propagating his faith by word of mouth all the way.

Islam is not notably intolerant. All colonials should know the safe-conduct given by El Bakay, of Timbuctoo, to Barth when he was returning to Bornu in 1855.

'Your guest is our guest, Abd el Kerim Barth the Christian . . . do not be led into error by those who say: "See, he is a Christian! Show him no friendship, rather do him evil so that you may please God." But such principles are contrary to the Koran and the Sunna and deserve the contempt of enlightened men. . . . Mahomet said "Whenever an honourable man approaches you receive him honourably", and himself, adding example to precept, received graciously all who came to him, whether they were Moslems or Bible sectaries (Jews or Christians). . . . As for the inoffensive infidel, there is no rule against treating him in a friendly manner; on the contrary, indeed, we are formally enjoined to treat him justly. To your wise men, learned and hospitable, who exercise authority and rule in your countries, to all of you, greeting and blessing. Verily my guest is your guest, and has nothing to fear from you because you obey God. . . .'

To Moslems, Christians, '*Nazarenes*', are men of the Book, unbelievers but not barbarians; pagans, on the contrary, are not worthy of the same respect. This value judgment is universal. In 1934 the

THE SPHERE OF THE DIVINE 101

medical students at the Native School of Medicine at Dakar were indignant when I asked if they still adhered to the fetishism in which they had been reared. They went to church, or to the temple or the mosque, or to a masonic lodge or nowhere at all, but none of them had remained faithful to fetishism, which they regarded as inferior to other religions or philosophies.

An hypothesis has been put forward which needs to be verified: the preaching of Islam has strengthened the influence of the secret societies among the pagans. In any district where both mosques and sacred groves are found, if a fanatical Moslem prophet should appear the administrator would need to keep an eye not only on the mosques but also on the sacred groves. For the defensive reaction of the pagans against a revival of Islam is to take refuge in mystery, to conceal their fetishes, to draw the initiates closer together in the use of their pre-scribed language, the practice of secret rites, the carrying out of redemptive sacrifices and the consultation of diviners. The Moslem, telling his beads aloud in the mosque, will not fail to react in his own way, and will inform the Commandant that there are sorcerers in the district terrorizing the villages. It would be interesting to know what part is played by Moslems in the denunciations of leopard-men and sorcerers.

In its relations with fetishism Islam is often the oppressor—it no longer wages a holy war by force of arms, but an economic war no less inimical to liberty. In the Kong area of the Ivory Coast, Moslems held a monopoly in the weaving of cotton cloth—a key industry—and they used the power this gave them to extend their supremacy and their propaganda. Pagan pedlars, wishing to ply their trade profitably, realize the advantages of getting themselves circumcized and mum-bling Koranic prayers. In the territory of Diourbel in Senegal an Islamic fraternity, the Mourides, is colonizing new land as far as Saloum, and systematically evicting and expropriating the pagan owners of the soil. The community is highly organized under the authority of an infallible marabout who lives in a corrugated-iron monastery and is building the finest mosque in French West Africa. One of its tenets is the necessity for tilling the soil and acquiring European techniques and implements; its members are sent out in search of fresh land, like the monks who first cleared the soil in Europe. A considerable proportion of the groundnuts exported from Diourbel and Kaolack depends on their labour, as does the com-mercial prosperity of French West Africa and the balancing of its budget. Naturally the Government welcomes the financial results of

102 FREEDOM AND AUTHORITY IN FRENCH WEST AFRICA

this activity and does not enquire too closely into the growth of Islam which accompanies it.

This may well be a more serious danger than the furious hostility of the Mahommedans towards the colonists in the old days. Gilbert Vieillard,[1] in his introduction to the Fulani poems of the Moslems of Fouta-Djallon in French Guinea, writes: 'We tear them from the contemplative life of the monk and the shepherd. . . . They display the natural reaction of ninth-century theologians suddenly invaded by positivist Martians.'

The following is an extract from these poems, composed in 1900–10 and admirably translated by Gilbert Vieillard:

Our sorrowful age

Now those who were destined one day to possess this country have entered into possession, and they are ruling there, but they do not follow the right path.

They put down the men of worth and exalt the worthless; and if even our Lords tremble before them, what of the poor peasants?

They have risen up against God's holy religion; they will not prosper. . . .

From the rage of the unbelievers O Lord deliver us!

Destroy the European throughout all Fouta; cast him out of Fouta, O thou our Help.

Destroy, root out the European through all our Fouta; cast him out of Fouta, O thou our Help.

Against those who devour taxes

The Mahdi, whose hour we await, will come and bring succour to religion; he will take arms against the devourers of taxes and drive them into the next world.

Let us accept the French

This world is a camp; a camp is not a home; so many others, before the French, pitched their tents and went on their way.

THE ADMINISTRATOR MUST BE SECULAR

It is absolutely essential—though it is difficult—for the administrator to maintain a secular standpoint in dealing with different religions. I am well aware of the first objection that will be raised: that colonial practice will be immoral if it is not inspired by the religion of the colonist. But then, what is to happen to the religions of the colonized? It is the duty of the administrator to see that liberty of conscience is respected, to stand for tolerance and to hold the

[1] *Comité d'études historiques et scientifiques de l'A.O.F.* Bulletin 3, 1937 (Juillet-Septembre). Gilbert Vieillard, assistant administrator in the colonial service, died in battle in France, in June 1940, when serving as a gunner-sergeant.

THE SPHERE OF THE DIVINE 103

balance between the temporal interests of the different religions. The real question is whether, in exercising the art of political administration—an art which, as I have said, involves the whole personality of the man who practises it—it is either right or possible for that personality to stop short at the threshold of the Divine. Can an administrator, whether he is a practising Catholic or a convinced Protestant, think otherwise than as a Christian? Will he not, by surrendering his personality, rob his profession of its vital quality?

I believe that an administrator can preserve his freedom and maintain the secular standpoint in his profession if he keeps the following rules:

Every religion is to be respected, but no religion can require the administrator to act as its secular agent or its clerical assistant.

In order to arbitrate between their secular interests he must understand their spiritual evolution, penetrating beyond the customary observances which often represent a debased form; but it is on the spiritual level that he must refuse to intervene.

The secular status of the Administration cannot exist without a separation of State and Church, or if there is idolatry or worship of the State. An administrator need not be an atheist in order to be secular, but he must not deify the State or Progress or any particular form of civilization or any myth such as the notion of race.

In practice the art of the administrator will consist in persuading religious personages that relations between religion and government must be ruled by a system of arbitration on which the parties have agreed. Disputes should not arise between individuals, one representing Cæsar and the other God; a method of arbitration must be organized.

This thing seems simple, but it is in fact most difficult to carry out successfully. In all good faith—literally speaking—a believer thinks his faith should embrace everything—even the most mundane affairs. As if it were the most natural thing in the world, he will expect the administrator to foster religious enterprises, to take special measures for the protection of their goods and premises, to order the chiefs to assist the newly converted, and to delegate to the missionaries of his religion administrative authority over the chiefs themselves.

It is very necessary, therefore, that the competence of the administrator should be clearly defined by means of written regulations and a judicial procedure for regulating disputes, particularly in regard to territorial concessions, rights of association and education. The State often fails to carry out this duty.

104 FREEDOM AND AUTHORITY IN FRENCH WEST AFRICA

This is because the task is a difficult one. The State uses a vocabulary full of vague abstractions. It goes so far as to say (Art. 22 of the Covenant of the League of Nations) that 'the welfare and development of dependent peoples constitute a sacred mission of civilization'. But when it comes to including in the functions of the administrator anything more than a vague religiosity—such as this 'sacred' mission of civilization—the State stops short, as if afraid to finish off completely the native societies which it has nevertheless mortally wounded.

Let us consider its attitude to the problem of the family, which, according to Wilbois[1] is 'the whole social problem'. The African family is built on a complex of customs, the core of which is polygamy, and the structure of which has a geometrical regularity. Wilbois formulates them thus:

> Fundamental axiom: Man is essentially superior to woman.
> Theorem 1. Woman cannot live without man.
> Corollary 1. A widow is inherited by her husband's heir.
> Corollary 11. If the heir is already married he becomes a bigamist.
> Theorem 11. Only women have to work.
> Corollary 1. If a woman works she represents wealth.
> Corollary 2. If she represents wealth, it is necessary to pay a price for marrying her.
> Corollary 3. Anyone who is rich enough will have several wives.

Wilbois then proposes the following principles of action:

1st principle. The two sexes should be regarded as equal, even if the man exercises the authority.

2nd principle. The single household, rather than the group of households, is the real social unit.

3rd principle. No woman ought to be given in marriage for any consideration—either handed over or promised—which may be regarded as, or could be converted into, a purchase price.

4th principle. The ideal household is monogamous and indissoluble.

Pending the general acceptance of these principles, Wilbois suggests that the following four points should be insisted on immediately:

> 1. Girls can not be promised in marriage before they reach the age of puberty.

---

[1] Joseph Wilbois. *L'Action sociale en pays de Missions,* Payot, 1938. See also L. Barde's comments in the *Dossiers de l'Action populaire,* 10 fev. 1939.

THE SPHERE OF THE DIVINE 105

2. A girl can not be married without her consent.
3. A widow shall not legally belong to her husband's heir.
4. Polygamy shall be combatted as rapidly as possible.

'Polygamy', says Wilbois, 'is manifested as a powerful and insidious tyranny which the average Christian cannot resist by means
of the prayers and sacraments which are efficacious against ordinary
temptations.' To which L. Barde adds the comment: 'The law, which
relies on new forms of behaviour born of Christianity and which
fosters their diffusion, must in short smooth the path to virtue.'

Whether it is the duty of the State to promote the service of God
is a very large question. In fact, since the law is silent on the matter,
there will inevitably be a conflict between the missionary who, in the
words of L. Barde, 'acts not as the practitioner of a cult but as a giver
of life to the world', and the administrator who also has to give life
to a world but who has to permit polygamy because he feels himself
responsible for a social order of which polygamy is the basis.

With regard to Wilbois's first three points, the administrator has
simply to apply the declaration of the Rights of Man in defence of
the human person. As regards the fourth point—polygamy, he will
help Africans to build a new order where the polygamous family will
be replaced by the monogamous household.

With regard to the first three points, our position is not an intermediate one, half-way between unbelief and religion, it is a judicial
position. As for the fourth point, we are bound, as secular officials,
to recognize the practice of polygamy—but we are also bound to
think out new courses of action, and to build up, as a corporate
undertaking, a new African society in which the dignity of the human
person will be respected in the woman as in the man.[1] By what
method? This must be judicial and has been indicated in the previous
chapter: let custom evolve in the hands of the younger generations.

---

[1] Denise Moran, author of *Tchad*, who has recently returned from a prolonged
tour in A.O.F. will shortly publish the results of her enquiry. She is not a religious
and it will be interesting to compare her conclusions with those of Sister Marie-
André of the Sacred Heart in her *La Femme Noire en Afrique Orientale* (Payot
1939).

VIII. THE PEASANT COMMUNITY

IN 1931 I published my *Paysans Noirs*. The book made its reputation by its title. It introduced into the colonial vocabulary a more accurate term than the locutions 'native masses' or 'local labour force' which had been thought adequate to describe human beings. In contrast to Man, with a capital M, which seemed a merely rhetorical term, to be applied from outside, and the anonymous wretches of the 'collectivity' or the 'labour force', who nevertheless represented the only inner reality, the term 'black peasants' had a humanistic flavour and was found acceptable. It gave an outlet to a certain sentimental feeling for former slaves, while it reassured the modern slavers who had at first been a little anxious. Peasants—no danger there; one can go on in the old way. And what an alibi! What could be more bucolic? Instead of dealing in cotton or niggers, one can go in for black peasants.

It won't be so easy. True 'they' do not amount to much, naked and denuded in a harsh land. But such as they are, they are no longer unknown, and can no longer be disposed of as in the past. Is it proposed to tear them away from their villages? It will be necessary to provide superior surroundings. We shall promise to treat them well, and promise ourselves that they will be treated so scientifically that they will not know that they are being enslaved. They will not be carried off for any private enterprise, but for a government scheme of colonization, which will be in fact a state within a state. They will enter into the colonial condition like novices entering religion. We shall even call mystical sanctions to our aid to induce faith in them. Generous supplementary grants will of course be needed for propaganda and police, a more restrained note in prophecies of prosperity, incessant displays and parades, and a better fitting mask. Literature will thereby be enriched by the figure of a slave trader far more subtle in character than those of the time when we liberated the Niger.

The simple term 'black peasant' is not the whole truth. Money, roads, the army, schools and the cross have disintegrated the social sructure in which the tillers of the soil were enclosed and until recently entrenched. The real task of the Administration, the real art of

THE PEASANT COMMUNITY

government, is not so much to deaden the impact of the forces of colonization as to discover with the peasants, and in them, the conditions of a new equilibrium for their lives. There is no question of staging a spectacular historical reconstruction, or dreaming of recalling the ancient Africa. The African peasant is the foundation of the new African society. Far from being a mere supernumerary, dressed up and made use of, he is the central point of the administration and the determining factor in its experimental methods; he demands a territorial administration and he is its inspiration.

He has to be approached from within, as it were, but this cannot always be achieved at the outset. His individual qualities vary with climate and locality. The *talakkas* of the Niger are not the same people as the *gletanou* of Dahomey or the *badolo* of Saloum. Nevertheless, they have common characteristics. In the first place that unspoken suspicion of masters and foreigners which in itself would suffice to make them kin to peasants the world over. It disguises itself as indifference, stupidity, inertia. The peasants I have had to do with only surrendered to me at last after lengthy overtures. If I call them to mind to-day, they are still withdrawn; speechless they emerge from their far-off fields in the bush, from the huts which shoulder one another in the homesteads and from those curious underground or terraced fortifications which are the granaries of the whole village.

They glide along, appearing without a word, in their cotton rags, with their basket-work and their pottery and their primitive iron tools. They seem so defenceless on their poor exhausted soil, which nevertheless in the rainy season exhales a fragrance of vigour and a promise of fruitfulness.

What do I know of them? That they have already forced us to reconsider the powers of native chiefs, to establish the legal status of villages and to undertake a reorganization of Africa at a deep level. This peasantry is constituting itself a peasant community. Its property has not been surveyed and registered, but its members have been identified. Already they are regrouping themselves in economic associations which sooner or later will have political significance.

Their title to property, which is inseparable from their person, is simply the title of peasant. So that we may continue to govern, that is, to serve them, I wish to show why this peasantry has not been recognized, how it has been exploited, the methods by which it has been understood, and by what means and to what ends the peasant community is being built up.

108 FREEDOM AND AUTHORITY IN FRENCH WEST AFRICA

IT EXISTED BEFORE THE COLONIAL ERA

When the slaver of the present day leans his elbows on the Minister's desk, fixes him with his eyes, bombards him with statistics and asserts that he himself has created the peasant, he is ballyhooing in the blue. The peasants are not the whole of Africa, but at all events they were there before he was. Africa has had kingdoms and empires, and, as we have seen, these were political constructions based and built up on villages. The Soudanese 'hegemonies', as Delafosse terms them, were simply a pyramid of villages. And what is a village but the expression of a peasantry?

In the days of the kingdom of Benin or the empires of Ghana, Malik or the Askias, African economy was agricultural. There is no evidence of industries or mines which might have supported a State. The only resources of the sovereign resided in the peasants. These vast territorial hegemonies could only have existed because rural life was sufficiently ample and well organized to support them. If there were armies it was because the villages produced enough grain to feed the cavalry which was the chief military force. Do not let us picture those days as a golden age. We used to think that Africa before we came there was nothing; we should not go to the other extreme and imagine that thanks to a powerful peasant community it possessed everything. The peasants were decimated by wars and famines, although they tried to secure themselves by storing grain in good years: for reserve granaries existed before European administration.

There is other evidence for the existence of the peasantry: though the colonists did not recognize it, explorers had discovered it. To cite only four of the nineteenth-century explorers, Caillié, Barth, Binger and Monteil all describe the African peasant at work. As late as 1929 a pamphlet, published by the Government of French West Africa for publicity purposes, described as a backward people the cultivators of the Korogho region whom Monteil had observed in full activity thirty years earlier, in 1891. The records of nineteenth-century travellers throw into strong relief the rural activity and the organized agriculture of that Africa which had been bled for two and a half centuries by the slave trade and whose ancient agricultural civilization had had to bend before the blast of a religion of nomads, horsemen and camel-drivers: Islam.

Why Unrecognized?

At first everything conspired to prevent the earliest colonizers from recognizing the African peasantry. The geographical location of the black peasant upsets all our preconceived ideas. It is obviously not the desert, nor the dense forest, and can only be the steppe or the savanna. But even in the savanna there is at first sight no trace of cultivation. In the dry season the savanna appears to be uncultivated; it unrolls itself like a shaggy carpet, bristling with thorn, bumpy with ant-hills and embellished with arcades of trees along the water-courses. And in the smoky atmosphere of burnt-out fires, in which the flames of bush fires still flicker, the European cannot detect any farmland. But if he flies over this same country in the rainy season he will see from the plane a pattern of furrows, hillocks and level fields —as if, all of a sudden, the peasants had arisen and quickened the earth. They have left the village and gone—sometimes as much as a two days' journey—to camp in the fields and make a new village there, called the farming village. They bring dead wood and scatter it in little heaps which they burn to get potash. They clear the ground of stones and stumps and loosen the soil before getting together in teams to begin the first tillage. Sometimes they point out to us the sites of former fields and explain their system of shifting cultivation. What we thought was bush was really a stretch of fallow-land. We have not as yet thoroughly studied native land utilization. Is it strip cultivation? A survey should be made by a geographer of this system of working small parcels of land, intermittent but recurring. But already the administrator has perceived, not a continent of primitive savagery nor yet a blank and bare expanse, but an archipelago of islands in the bush where rural life revolves in an annual cycle of fallows and cultivation.

It is no less difficult to perceive the peasant himself. At first he was concealed by his overlords. Most of the great chiefs with whom the Europeans first came into contact on the economic or political level, were not bound by any close ties to the peasantry they ruled. They were Tuaregs, Moors, Fulani—that is to say Semites who reigned over the negroes; they were nomads or pastoralists who exercised authority over sedentary cultivators; they were Moslems who had enslaved fetishists, theologians who despised illiterate pagans. They formed a screen between us and the peasants. And in our earliest colonizing days they succeeded in persuading the peasant that he was

110   FREEDOM AND AUTHORITY IN FRENCH WEST AFRICA

unfit to approach us or communicate with us. There is a proverb of the Kong district which is significant: 'Only Moslems know how to talk to the French'. And in fact, under the French, just as before the French, the Moslem Dyulas exercised political power and kept the pagan Senufo in bondage.

Invisible and oppressed, the African peasantry suffered an extremity of wretchedness which has never been estimated. Let us stress again: two and a half centuries of the slave trade and, even in the nineteenth century, the depredations of a conqueror like Samory, strangled the breath of life in the villages.

While European trade made its way into Africa and reached the chiefs, the lot of the peasant grew worse. As the use of money spread and chiefs were able to buy imported goods, the peasant had to work even harder with no gain to himself. Whether he was a slave in the chief's household or a serf in a village dependent on the chief, he began to suffer from the effects of the economic disequilibrium; he worked too hard in relation to his technical equipment and at the expense of his family and social life, but not hard enough to satisfy the needs of the chief. As long as he had to produce only so much grain that a part of the harvest, converted into cowries, would purchase for the chief a spear or a horse, his servitude was more or less endurable. But when, in the same conditions and with the same tools, he had to produce enough to enable the chief to pay in bank-notes for a car and a gun, then all the harvest was absorbed and his burden became intolerable.

But even when we became aware of the peasant behind his chiefs and beneath his wretchedness, misunderstandings between him and ourselves were not at an end. We were confronted by a being to whom our feelings were sympathetic but of whom our reason could not approve. We went to him armed with diplomas in agriculture, ready to organize him scientifically in his work, but he did not understand us; we thought his knowledge of his soil and his calling was merely habitual practice. And he did not encourage our attempts to help him. Above all, his wretched equipment and his curious methods made us doubt whether he really was a peasant. We had come, almost all of us, from the Europe of towns, the France of cities; we had been brought up with a very literary notion of agricultural life. From the time of Virgil at least the peasant had been a classical figure whose attributes were oxen and the plough. Oxen and ploughs seemed part of the natural order of the soil. In Africa there were no ploughs and no oxen except in herds. How then could there be peasants? On the

THE PEASANT COMMUNITY

other hand we were already indoctrinated with the notion peculiar to industrial Europe of the nineteenth century, the notion of output.

To our minds, labour necessarily implied efficient equipment; these people whom we found tilling the soil in Africa had for equipment a sickle, an axe and a more or less substantial hoe. And their output? An annual crop barely sufficient to keep the village from starvation till the next harvest, providing nothing for the market.

As for their agricultural system, it was a complete mystery to us. We knew, of course, that at one time French peasants had practised a system of fallows and even a sort of shifting cultivation, but then they were already organized on a basis of individual ownership. But African villages, or so it appeared, combined a system of fallows with communal ownership of land. The fact was that their social organization was one most alien to our ways of thought, being thoroughly communal. That, of course, was a narrow and mistaken view. Actually, within the collectivity as we saw it, family rights in property did exist, and within the family unit there was personal ownership. But it was important to recognize that the family, whether patriarchal or matriarchal, was not confined to one couple but included all the descendants of a common ancestor, not only the living but the dead also, and not only human beings but animals possessing protective functions. With regard to family property a sort of 'tacit communalism' functioned, analogous, according to Labouret, to that practised in the Niverne country in the sixteenth century where 'men ate from the same pot and worked together'. But within the family, certain rights devolved on individuals. For instance, if an individual member of the community makes something by his own labour—a rice field, a rough stone wall round a mountain pasture—he has a lively sense of his own proprietary rights in it.

Not only was the system of land tenure unintelligible to us, but their methods of tillage defeated us. For instance, there was the communal working party of young people of the same age group, collected from neighbouring villages to work in the same field; girls worked on one side of it, boys on the other, all drawn up in line, bent over their hoes, jumping backwards at the word of command to drive the hoe into the ground between their legs, thus moving in formation obliquely across the field and tracing a multiple furrow as they went. This seemed to us a spectacle of ethnological interest—but not agriculture. With our background of European individualism, we did not perceive that Africa had succeeded in combining family forms of ownership with communal methods of labour.

112 FREEDOM AND AUTHORITY IN FRENCH WEST AFRICA

In family forms and communal methods alike breathed a religious spirit which seemed to us mere superstition. No inheritance of property without sacrificial rites, no labour without prayers and incantations. Much more serviceable to African agriculture than draught animals is the animal which is killed in order to discover whether the right field has been chosen, whether the work can be done, and the harvest ensured. 'My God,' says the Mossi peasant, 'I give you this fowl; in exchange, help me to get millet. Making the millet grow, harvesting and eating it are the three things which keep the world going. God, I give you this fowl so that you may help me in these three things.' We came from an industrialized Europe, where the factories are joyless affairs, and found people who worked to music. Communal labour had its drums and tom-toms, its orchestras to cheer the workers on. And we asked ourselves: 'Are they working or enjoying themselves? Their tools are ludicrous and they don't even use them seriously.'

And the last cause of the peasants' wretchedness and of the misunderstandings between them and us is the yearly struggle to make ends meet. In Africa there often have to be two or three sowings to get one harvest and the harvest barely suffices for one year's needs. And when the time of the heaviest farm work comes round the peasant can eat only once a day. He has to work hardest at the very time when he eats least and when his strength is at its lowest.

And so we were unprepared to understand the African peasants. The French peasants, at a cost in misery which we no longer remember, have made of France a garden in which rare islands of wilderness still persist. The African peasant, on the contrary, occupies a few islands of cultivated land in an encircling ocean of bush. Moreover, these islands are not all the same: traditional forms of work and property vary according to the area and the kind of cultivation. The whole situation was so different from what we had expected that we sometimes even denied to these people the status of peasants; we did not realize how they must have laboured and suffered to make their soil into cultivable land, and we regarded them as merely labourers, only fit to be used on European plantations.

The Exploitation of the Peasantry

First of all we used them to open up their country. All major undertakings—railways, roads, ports—were carried out by the conscription of peasant labour. If French West Africa to-day possesses a skeleton

THE PEASANT COMMUNITY   113

of highways and a nervous system of commercial and administrative cities, it is because peasants, taken on as labourers, have left their fields to make roads—60,000 kilometres of them—and their villages to build towns. A task necessary in itself but which has weighed heavily on them because it has been carried out by compulsion. This is the slaver's pretext for claiming that the Administration is his secret accomplice. From what was formerly the Upper Volta, a colony of three million peasants, the Government of French West Africa took 25,276 labourers between 1920 and 1924 for building the railway from Thiés to the Niger, 42,830 between 1921 and 1930 for timber cutting and work in the plantations of the Ivory Coast. Over a period of ten years 84,107 have had to serve far from their own homes, a thousand kilometres away to the west, 500 to the south. In the colony itself, from 1927 to 1929, 42,313 have been requisitioned for public works and 52,416 for work on commercial sites. On the basis of these official figures[1] we can say that between 1920 and 1930 nearly 189,000 able-bodied men in the prime of life, representing the best twentieth of the population, have been torn from their families, from marriage,[2] from the villages and from the fields.

Those heads of subdivisions, Commandants of *cercles*, and Governors, who wanted to arrest this flowing away of the peasantry, were suspected of disloyalty and deprived of means of action. They were compelled to look on helplessly while the territories in their charge were bled white. They saw the resurgence, in modern form, of the serfdom and slavery which they thought to have cured. The temporary Governor of the Ivory Coast, Richard Brunot, who denounced forced labour and organized voluntary work, was recalled and disgraced. Apparently he was asked if he thought he was Jesus Christ.

No, we did not think we were Jesus Christ. We were simply administrators who wanted to do our job of administration.

The great evil we had to deal with was the misunderstanding of labour conscription. In 1922, as a young assistant administrator in the Niger Colony, I heard our Governor, M. Brévié, remind us of the proper rules of conscription. In 1937, the Governor General, Marcel de Coppet, stated them again. They can be summed up under two heads:

    1. No conscription of labour apart from the requirements of public

---

[1] Published on the occasion of the 1931 exhibition.

[2] The results are beginning to show: the birth rate is falling in the Ouagadougou and Bobo districts and in general in all the former territories of the Upper Volta. Recruiting of young men and men in the prime of life for the army, public works, private enterprise and the *Navetane* migration reduced the so-called reserve of man-power in French West Africa to a dangerous condition of stagnation.

114 FREEDOM AND AUTHORITY IN FRENCH WEST AFRICA

works, which shall be discussed by the council of elders of the district, approved by the Governor and carried out by the Administration.

2. Every adult male who is liable shall give, in money or personal service, at the most ten days' work, which may be done at one or at different times and when he is not needed for work in the fields. If he has to travel more than five kilometres from his village to the place of work, he will be fed by the Administration.

These are excellent rules and should be sufficient to prevent conscription of labour being turned into forced labour. But M. de Coppet points out that the rules are constantly broken by the extension of the number of days beyond ten, by the employment of women and children, and by the distance of the working sites, which are sometimes not five kilometres but five days' walk away, and where the people are not provided with food.

What is the reason for this? Marcel de Coppet gives it with a frankness[1] which was no less unpardonable in him than it was in Richard Brunot: a certain Commandant has a network of 500 kilometres of roads to maintain on a credit of 10,000–15,000 francs, which just allows him to buy shovels and picks and to make a few payments in compensation. What will he do? Exactly what one expects. He will override the regulations in order to meet the demand for well-kept roads, comfortable camps and perfect airfields.

If the 60,000 kilometres of highways, the urban centres and the airfields are to be maintained without recourse to these methods, the 118 Commandants of French West Africa would need to avail themselves of a system other than that of forced labour; as Boisson, the acting Governor General said in 1938, a credit of 800 millions would be necessary. How could this sum be provided out of a total budget of 1,312 millions?

Conscripted labour simply has to be used. The problem is how to keep it within limits, and not allow it to overflow, as it has done for so many years, into a stream of abuses which infect public works, react on private enterprises and destroy villages.

[1] Now that Governor-General de Coppet has left West Africa, after having borne insults and hatred like a gentleman, it is good to recall that because of the deep sympathy he inspired in native circles he was able to achieve the extraordinary recruitment of artillerymen in June and December, 1938. Can it be said that his ideas and actions regarding forced labour damaged the prosperity of French West Africa? One fact is sufficient answer to this. For the colonies of Senegal and the Ivory Coast, economically the most important of the group, 1937 and 1938 were, under de Coppet's governorship, record years for both export and import tonnage. Thus in this French West Africa, said to be full of disturbances, the leader whom people wished to discredit because he defended the natives was getting discipline and work from them.

THE PEASANT COMMUNITY

Let us understand the situation properly. The organization of labour in French West Africa has been the subject of wise regulations which, since 1937, have been embodied in a code. But how many workers really come under the code? In 1935, for example, 30,700 were recruited by contract, for administrative undertakings, or for private enterprise of the European type; 38,900 labourers were requisitioned for urgent work of general importance which required a total of 172,000 days. The spirit of this labour code permeates the relations between employer and worker in the case of 255,300 men employed without contract on sites and in private enterprise. But they are only a minority. The regulations and accepted customs *only protect about 325,000 men. There remains a majority of 3,318,000 peasant-labour conscripts who owe in theory 21,187 million workdays and whose rights are abused because the rules concerning them are not applicable.* It is in this respect that the peasants are exploited and the peasant community threatened. Here is the evil which, if it is not extirpated, demoralizes the Administration and exhausts the country.

The technique of administration has its own morality—a code of ethics proper to itself. If an administrator, in this machine age, has to build a road for heavy motor traffic and can use only forced labour unequipped with tools, a breach of taste has been committed which will have far-reaching results. The territory will suffer for it and sooner or later the evil will break out.

No improvements in hygiene, no demographic progress are possible in so far as endemic and epidemic diseases are in fact products of forced labour; their primary cause is the failure of resistance, the social disequilibrium of the peasant conscript, the victim of forced labour. True, roads bring the doctor to him, but since they have been built by force, disease is the first traveller on them and they have struck from the hands of the peasant his real shield—his fields.

Built by force—let us stress it again. These are the conditions in which we have had to administer and govern. The diabolic slaver made the development of the country and economic necessity his pretexts. The situation of the colony is such that the native territories have to export in order to provide the money to meet their own needs. In order to forge the whole structure of headquarters and territorial stations, to connect up communications, to equip schools and dispensaries, there must be budgets, trade, exports.

Moreover, the African territories are so placed that export crops are produced in the coastal regions which are relatively underpopulated, whereas concentrations of population are found in the Soudan

116   FREEDOM AND AUTHORITY IN FRENCH WEST AFRICA

where crops are unsuitable for export either by nature or because of their remote situation. To ensure to French West Africa as a whole a sufficient revenue for administrative costs, economic development and social services, Soudanese peasants have to travel to the coast to cultivate export crops: groundnuts in Senegal, cocoa on the Ivory Coast. They have, in fact, done so and have become pioneers of a new form of agriculture.[1]

The groundnut plantations are the property of native Senegalese and are cultivated on the *metayage* principle, whereby the labourers work in the morning for the owners and in the afternoon for themselves. (There is no European-owned groundnut industry in Senegal.) The cocoa plantations of the Ivory Coast are becoming to an ever-increasing extent the property of the local native middle class which is now arising. European colonials in banana-growing Guinea and in the cocoa and coffee-growing Ivory Coast are now surrounded by native-owned plantations which, according to Professor Chevalier, are not badly managed. Here are some figures: in 1935, out of total exports valued at 700 million francs, 635 million were produced by native cultivation.

Moreover, the peasantry, while bearing the burden of opening up the country, and providing the seasonal migration of labour to produce the export crops, has still managed to sustain an internal economy for which no reliable statistics are available, but which by innumerable channels maintains a flow of petty trading and keeps the pulse of rural life and labour beating.

For 65,000 hectares of European plantations there are $2\frac{1}{2}$ million square kilometres under native cultivation. Food production in French West Africa is entirely the work of the black peasant.

The Commandants Understood

Peasant labour had to be understood in order that, wretched as it was, it should not be debased; it had to be studied on the spot, in the country where it still drew on the living forces of the past, where it was still expressed in terms of persons and where the administrator was brought face to face with men. Confronted by this vicious system which was crushing the peasant, we—chiefs of subdivisions, commandants of *cercles* and a few governors—did not take our stand

[1] The migrations of the groundnut *Navetanes* from the Soudan to Senegal are as follows: 1933, 33,540; 1934, 29,540; 1935, 41,620; 1936, 55,500; 1937, 45,300; 1938, 74,000. Migrations of cocoa labour, from the Soudan area to the Ivory Coast and Gold Coast number about 100,000 per annum.

THE PEASANT COMMUNITY 117

on a theoretical morality; we did not throw away the baby with the bath-water. In our tours, in our daily life in the territory we had diagnosed the malady and, as practising administrators we sought, not to construct a doctrine, but to discover the springs of action in the peasant organism.

What gadfly was biting us? The old revolutionary struggle against the slavers? A breath from our own French country-side, and its age-ing and neglected fields, urging us to save the fields of an African France and of French Africans? Disgust at the disharmony between official words and official actions? The desire to be able to act with a clear conscience? All these perhaps, but above all the fact that we were not professors but practitioners and that we were conscious of the necessity and the possibility of understanding these people with whom we lived.

Reforms were introduced later on which aimed at giving the African peasantry the status of a peasant community, but these were not dropped from on high by the General Staff.[1] On the contrary it was the territorial administration which shepherded them, by slow and painful stages from the bush to headquarters, after trying them out by private researches. To give only three examples in the Soudan area alone: The production of cotton at Diré, rice at Mopti, ground-nuts at Bobo-Dioulasso enabled the Commandants to prove that the local peasantry could produce on a large scale and without compulsion, if they were convinced that it was to their interest to do so, and if their traditional methods of working were understood and respected.

The following observations on the agricultural cycle of the Gouin of Bobo-Dioulasso district were made in 1928-9:

1. *Choice of new farming land.* There is not much new land in this area. Almost all suitable land has been or is being cultivated. In certain districts there is indeed a shortage of land and people have to lease it at some distance away, paying rent in corn or in cash.

There are three kinds of property: communal or village property, in which the village, represented by the headman, exercises protective and regulative rights. This generally applies to land on which fruit is gathered; manorial ownership, that is, land belonging to the chief of the canton and the village chief; family property, *soukhala*, for the

[1] It was French West Africa's good fortune that the General Staffs had at their head Governors who supported, co-ordinated and developed the experiments made by administrative officers.

118 FREEDOM AND AUTHORITY IN FRENCH WEST AFRICA

use and habitation of the household. If the head of a family wishes to bring a part of the bush into cultivation, or to make a fallow or bring back into cultivation land which has not been worked for some time, he consults the land chief. The land chief may be the village headman. He watches over the land of the village like a guardian angel or like one who performs a ritual act.

The head of the family inspects the land which has been allotted to him. He sacrifices a chicken to the spirits of the ancestors and to the local gods, either in his home or in the sacred grove behind his farm or on the land itself. He visits the diviner who carries out a fresh sacrifice. If all the sacrifices are favourable, if the chicken 'falls right' (on its back) the choice is made. In fact the land chief, the head of the family, and the diviner are all old peasants who can smell out good land; but it would be sacrilege to cultivate it without performing ritual actions.

2. *Cultivation.* First the clearing in the spring. All the men of the family cut down the bush with axes, root up the grass with picks, collect grass and bushes round a great tree and burn them. If necessary they remove stones. At the first rains they mark out the furrows with their hoes; after the rains they go over it burying the grass which has sprung up; this is the first manuring with vegetable matter. When the fields are worked over for the second time, the age groups come into play: the boy or married man who is reckoned the best worker of his age in his village begins the work in the field belonging to his family, the members of his age group, both men and women, working with him. Then they move off to the field belonging to that member of the group who was the first to answer the call of the best worker, and so on. The group includes a tom-tom player and two drummers of any age. The leading worker is accompanied by his sister or wife, and so are the others. Sometimes there are ten or more working, with the same number of women. The whole company forms itself into a line when the work starts; the line advances obliquely as the work progresses. The workers strike their hoes into the ground between their legs and move backward in jumps. The tom-tom player seems to push them back all the time.[1] Some of the fields cultivated by the group belong to members of the group, not to the head of the family. The sowing is done by a man, a woman or a child armed with a little basket full of seed and a stick to make holes with; the sower fills up the hole again with his foot. As soon as the green blades appear,

[1] Ten years after, in 1939, the great plain of Banfora was being ploughed with tractors belonging to the Native Provident Society.

THE PEASANT COMMUNITY 119

children come and keep watch. The age groups come into action for the weeding. Weeding is done twice with a small hoe, and they go over the field again with a large hoe to earth up the millet (in July–August). Women who do not belong to the group prepare food and take it to the labourers. For harvesting voluntary associations are formed. Three or four rows are marked out to be cut down to the ground with the weeding pick or small hoe. The women break off the cobs by hand and put them in baskets. The cobs are dried in heaps in the open air and the best are kept for seed and tied to a tree. The head of the family calls his neighbours to help thresh the grain, and the threshing is made the occasion for a feast. A sheep is killed and the new beer (*dolo*) is broached.

3. *Production:* Can the family produce on a large scale and make a profit? It can, if production on the new scale is tried out with one crop, while maintaining the traditional multi-crop cultivation at the same time. Large-scale production will then be as it were the surplus of family life. How can this production be stimulated and organized?

Methods for Stimulating and Organizing Production on a Family Basis.

(*a*) The Commandant studies the country in the Government records and on his tours, and explains it to those who are to work with him. He keeps an eye on the native chiefs so that they do not set up shop as brokers of the crop in question. He will not give any undertakings to commercial interests or allow any specified tonnage to be imposed on the territory beforehand. He controls the seed-corn and its distribution and use, and exercises that control when he goes on tour—one of those 'aimless' tours, described by van Vollenhoven, when he goes out without warning and chats with people about one thing and another. It is a good thing to know at least one man in each village by name and to have a new peg to hang the conversation on at each visit. It is of no consequence whether the Commandant displays irritation or amusement, the important thing is to be lively and to enliven. He has already cast his eye over the cultivated fields and formed an estimate of their condition, and when the moment is ripe, he speaks about an experiment he wants made. Certain fields are inspected and the record of sowings consulted; fantastic forecasts of probable yields are noted without comment. The peasants call this way of doing things 'playing cards' and they are pleased because a white man will play with them. So the proposed experiment is not

120 FREEDOM AND AUTHORITY IN FRENCH WEST AFRICA

just the white man's idea but a game in which they have an interest and which they will use some ingenuity to win.

It is very important to realize that the family will regard the experiment as a burden, so the Commandant must treat the family as a lever and suit the burden to the lever. Also, there must be music, native music and dancing, as well as that other music which is heard in the voice of the leader, speaking in palavers and on tour.

(b) Finally it is necessary to take care that these experiments and efforts are not interfered with. One of the plagues which afflicted production was Public Works as they often used to be carried out. Niggardly credits—the leavings of the annual estimates—no loans, no labour fund, little equipment; a few native workmen, a few European engineers. What could be done with that? For the Commandant the only really indispensable form of public works is road-making. Roads are useful for production and reduce the need for human porterage. There must be a permanent main road and trade roads in the dry season. In all weathers, and particularly in winter, the state of the permanent road will depend on the amount of traffic and the number of labourers impressed for road service. But even if credits are not forthcoming, it is possible to have one road mender per kilometre. He can mend the road in the neighbourhood of his village; he can fill up the hens' nests; if necessary he can recruit some of his friends. He is directly responsible to the Commandant who deals directly with him, and does not bother the village chief. Thus in regard to this colonial affair, a road, a healthy native reaction is set up, a native association of road-makers. There are some trivial things which save much distress: even if an important person is expected, there is no need to pull up the grass which in winter forms a protecting bank on each side of the road; there must be ditches alongside a road or else the rains will scoop out a bed in the middle of the carriage-way.

In the case of serious mishap—landslides, floods, breaking of the road surface—it is no use taking refuge in a report and calling for help from the office. The Commandant will have to collect labour as quickly as he can and carry out break-down repairs. He himself will merely have to act as traffic controller for the shop-keepers' lorries and prevent bottle-necks and blocking of the vital transport system; but an emergency equipment for break-down repairs will include huts, stores and cooks.

The dry-season trade roads will have to be made by labour gangs during the rainy season, because in Africa road-making requires

THE PEASANT COMMUNITY   121

water. In general this period is prohibited by the regulations, since the rainy season is thought to be the only time for farm-work. So the labour gangs are condemned to interminable fatigues of drawing water from wells and swamps, whereas in the rains water can be had for nothing.

Labour gangs should be set to work within the limits of the service period, and if their task is done before the appointed time, they should be released. Labour gangs should not be under the orders of guards, but of their natural chiefs and the heads of age-sets. Here also native society should be free to meet the colonial situation in its own way. Let the administrator come to terms with native society if he would make it accept the fact of colonial administration.

When private enterprises make demands for labour, often without rhyme or reason, the Commandant should apply the regulations and see to it that recruitment is voluntary. A reputable firm will ask for men and make permanent employees of them, and will not always be clamouring for 'porters', that is, unskilled labour. The word 'porter' conceals many evils; the porter is a peasant who works without tools, with no future, who bears for the white man the burden of the colonial Sisyphus. The question of labour on a large European plantation, provided with capital, equipment and organization, is a special case, and a complex one. Here, it seems, one can put one's faith in the colonial fact, which is strong and vital enough to absorb the native family and provide a new way of life; but this is rare.

(c) After all these precautions have been taken, numerous defects will become apparent; but the Commandant must not let himself be discouraged or deflected from his purpose. The really serious thing to-day is that the family is so often forced to subsist on the current year's harvest. The abundant stocks of millet, fruit of three years' harvesting, which heads of families used to lay up, no longer exist. In the famine season, when the maize and fonio are exhausted, hoeing falls off and no one works in the rice-fields. Just when the peasant has most work to do he has least to eat and the greatest number of pointless worries. He lives so far from his fields that cooking and sleeping are difficult, and he eats his food cold in the open field and sleeps there uncomfortably. If he is trying out a new crop on the good well-manured land which lies close to the farm and the village, it will be difficult to care for the traditional crops now relegated to distant fields, sometimes a day's walk away. And trifling irritations get on his nerves: the Administration has confiscated his flint-lock gun, so

122 FREEDOM AND AUTHORITY IN FRENCH WEST AFRICA

there will be no more game to eat, and monkeys pillage his field under his very nose.

Nevertheless, the land quickens and takes on new life. The villages are better kept, the people look more prosperous and wear a more confident air, and the greetings and the smiles which the peasants give to the Commandant are indications of his worth.

What about production? It can be proved that it exists, it is there in those poor huts. The question now is how to mobilize it.

(*d*) The term 'mobilization' itself suggests that the Administration has been prone to act with military severity in this matter. As agriculture has been subjected to a kind of military discipline, so markets have been militarized and produce requisitioned to stock them. Requisitioning is not necessarily baneful, but if it is applied under compulsion and through native intermediaries, its results are fatal to European commerce, which can never take root in the country by this method however delightful it seemed at first.

The traders maintain that without an order from the Commandant or the native chief no products are forthcoming. Does the African family then really refuse to co-operate? As a purchaser, possibly; but not as a vendor. The truth is simply that the African family is suspicious and cunning. The French peasant is equally suspicious of the Parisian tourist or the stranger who tries to buy milk and eggs in the village; and if the peasant is cunning enough to take refuge in 'official channels', he can gain time and stop up the channel.

The Commandants assert that if they do not act as wholesale agents for colonial products, that is, if they do not requisition, the merchants will do no business at all, or else will have dealings with the native chiefs and get them into trouble. And so the Commandant, in addition to all his other worries, has to undertake the transport, assembling, sharing out, weighing and paying the producers of commercial commodities.[1] He thinks that in this way he is assisting trade, while protecting and taming 'the native'.

The Public Works Department, the Commissariat, the Prisons, the Railway Workshops, all cry: 'The Commandant is the boss, the merchant is a useless and tiresome middleman, the native is an unknown quantity, so let the Commandant provide us with our necessary foodstuffs. Our ration returns are beautifully kept; the diets of porters and prisoners are accounted for to the last penny.' But the purchase of this food is organized by the Commandant or the native

---

[1] This militarism is bad for genuine trade, just as good planters sooner or later suffer from the system of forced labour, which only benefits bad ones.

THE PEASANT COMMUNITY 123

chief, and even though everything is carried out with the strictest honesty, there is always some unknown porter in the bush who carries loads without being paid for it, and there is always some peasant who has produced crops with no profit to himself and with no understanding of what happened. Finally, in town, there are ladies who telephone to the Commandant to ask for their daily chicken.

The results are appalling. If requisitioning is harshly carried out, and if it is aggravated by fixed maximum prices, it very quickly ruins both town and country. Even if it is not severe, it rouses opposition between country and town, and the prices of essential native products become so high that the cost of living rises, and the small official, European and native, becomes embittered.

Towns with 300 European inhabitants cannot live off a countryside of 300,000 peasants. Native-grown rice, for example, sells at a higher price than rice in France. The colonists get angry with the 'natives' and with their own profession which entails keeping up appearances and heavy expenses. They cannot manage to put by any savings, as was usual in the old days in the bush, because they have upset the economy of the country. But the position is still more serious, and a system of forced labour, unacknowledged but crushing in its effects, is disclosed. To supply the needs of the colonial population—industry, trade, the provisioning of the towns—the rural areas are drained of their resources and forced to produce commodities. And to effect this, all supplies have to be taxed, personal taxes increased and the prices of manufactured articles raised. As a result the markets are thronged, but only by the victims of forced labour, and often amount to traps laid to catch the peasants. Moreover, the colony is unhealthy; Africans and Europeans are equally 'weary', as the natives say, and equally discontented and become more and more incomprehensible to each other.

(e) When large-scale production of a given crop has been achieved by a native family, how is the crop to be conveyed to the colony, measured and paid for on a commercial basis, and so as to encourage the family to further efforts?

Native markets, accessible, at least in the dry season, to lorries, already exist in sufficient numbers to ensure that no village is more than one day's walk from a market. The Government, the Chamber of Commerce and the native councils should come to a joint arrangement whereby *one* private firm should begin the collection of commercial supplies. Quantities brought in should be measured accord-

124 FREEDOM AND AUTHORITY IN FRENCH WEST AFRICA

ing to some standard equally intelligible to peasants and Europeans thus avoiding the use of a weighing machine only. A measured amount which the peasant can *see* can afterwards be recorded by weight for the European accounting system; payment should be made at once, in cash, for each transaction. Or, alternatively, let the peasants organize a depot for the sale of their grain in these markets, by villages or wards or families, bringing in supplies by means of an endless chain of voluntary porters; let them appoint an overseer and keep some sort of tally of the numbers of measured units brought in for sale. On market days, European merchants will come and bid in free competition in the presence of the heads of families. The merchants, using the agreed measure, will empty the contents of the grain store into their lorries or silos and will reckon their payments with the aid of the tallies.[1] If the actual contents of the store do not correspond to the tally, the price of the actual contents will be handed to the overseer and the Commandant will be notified.

(*f*) What will be the effect on the family of its increased prosperity and its greater awareness of and co-operation with the colonial situation? It will become more and more individualist. The elders may sterilize tradition, but the younger generation will create a new tradition. This is becoming apparent in connection with marriages. Henceforth there will be money for the bride-price, though the bargaining may go on in the old way. But lovers overleap obstacles and evade tradition. They will found a new family, smaller and freer, which will be a better lever than the old one. And this new family will develop a critical spirit which it will be dangerous and impossible to stifle.

In matters of production and trade, indeed, villages near the main roads, and already 'advanced', are susceptible to the stimulus of competition and inducements to work, but are better able to distribute the basis of production and protect their own interests. To all appearances they produce less of any given commodity and are less docile than the remoter villages of the bush. But in fact they live better. And if the floating population which is attached to them were cleared out, their social order is better than that which exists in the bush.

But, young or old, the family will continue for a long time yet, in the intimacy of its home life, to place a quasi-religious ban on the

---

[1] Administrative officers may say ironically 'that's easy enough'. It is indeed not easy to humanize the impact of European trade on the traditional African economy. It is much easier to have recourse to forced labour and requisitions.

THE PEASANT COMMUNITY 125

white man. It is true that the young no longer think or behave in the same way as their elders, but the colonist will be grossly deceived if he imagines that either old or young will react in ways that correspond to European ideas. It is vital, and it is also sufficient, that the colonial system should be fruitful, and it is only by means of experiment that the European and the native components of that system can be continuously revealed to one another. The well-being of the colony is always a fragile and miraculous growth.

I do not claim that this account is exhaustive; I have not mentioned the place in the general picture of the prospective bridegrooms who work in the fields for the fathers of their brides, nor the importance of the iron-workers, the auxiliaries of agriculture. I have not discussed that 'social season' of the rains to which M. Tauxier has referred, and which embraces and includes the natural wet season. I have simply endeavoured to give an idea of the task of the administrative officer and his function in the training of the African peasant community.

The Building Up of a Peasant Community

A native policy based on local understanding and varied experimentation may form the basis for a general constructive programme which will combine four principal methods: the reconstitution of regional areas; the organization of the peasantry in these regions; their education; the provision of means of political expression.

1. *The reconstitution of regional areas:* a large programme of small public works.

The first step is to raise the peasants' standard of life in their own villages. This can be done in the villages as they are, and in their actual situation, in local conditions and by local means, so that the European spirit, instead of intervening to impose something ready made, will stimulate a spontaneous renewal. In each village we should seek to carry out, not spectacular constructions, but small works of public utility, such as a cemented well provided with a pump and a separate drinking trough for animals; or a granary protected from termites. Nothing much to look at, but providing a new benefit and a starting point for a better way of life in the village itself. This is what Marius Moutet called 'a large programme of small public works'. At the same time we should introduce small-scale mechanization adapted to the African outlook. An administrative officer, Valroff, invented a groundnut sheller and a cotton carder, two pieces of

126 FREEDOM AND AUTHORITY IN FRENCH WEST AFRICA

equipment which are both strong and simple, are easy to keep in order and can be worked by hand with movements that soon become habitual. Ives de Gall, a designer in a factory at Bamako, invented a loom which is an improved form of the traditional African loom. We invited French designers to construct a type of plough suitable for the light arable layer of African soil. Governor Poiret introduced two ploughs into French Guinea in 1913.[1] In 1938 there were more than 30,000 in French West Africa, not counting harrows and seed-drills. And oxen have been broken in, which is more of an achievement than might appear; it is easier to teach an African to drive a lorry than to use a plough, for the ox is not a machine and rural life is not a mechanical affair.

2. *Organizing the peasants:* From the family to producers' co-operatives and group marketing. Terms of agreement between the native co-operative and European commerce.

When it is re-established in its villages, the African peasant community has to be organized economically. From 1932 Governor General Brévié extended to the whole of French Africa the system of Native Provident Societies which had first been established in 1910 in Senegal. In 1931–2, when groundnut production fell far short of expectations, with a consequent loss of half the estimated revenues of French West Africa, means were sought to bring about a quick recovery and to reorganize production. It was essential to relieve producers of interest payments on loans of seed,[2] and to protect them against fluctuations in world prices. Production could be increased if producers were sure of not falling into debt and were guaranteed a remunerative selling price. The Government purchased 50,000 tons of seed and distributed it to cultivators through the agency of the Provident Societies. Groundnut production in Senegal was re-established in better conditions than before, and is now controlled by these native Societies.

All the heads of families in a district have to belong to the Society and pay an annual subscription of 10 sous to 3 francs according to the area.[3] The Society's assets are administered by a local council of notables, with the Commandant as chairman. What does the Society do with its money? It purchases selected seed, plants, and corn, and distributes them to its members, who have to repay it; it purchases agricultural machinery on the same terms; it sinks wells, builds store-

---

[1] The story of the African plough has been told by Governor Oswald Durant in *Terre Noir*, Librairie Fournier, 1935.

[2] In Sine-Saloum, Senegal, interest rates were as much as 300 per cent.

[3] Africans call this subscription 'the little tax', and there may be a danger here.

THE PEASANT COMMUNITY

houses; it settles peasants on new land for cultivation; it establishes experimental farms. In short, it deals with production.

It deals with sales also, and on the strength of a recent decree of the Council of State, it organizes collective sales for those of its members who desire it. The Society's intervention in the market results in the standardization of prices and a reduction in the middleman's profits. Here we have a basic organization of the agricultural peasant community which appeals alike to the old sense of community in the African peasant and the modern spirit of co-operation and organized labour. It is of course open to criticism, and some commercial interests have done so. Native Provident Societies must naturally beware of becoming government controlled; but co-operation is not the same as State control.

In Africa as elsewhere, and perhaps more easily than elsewhere, family ownership can evolve within a co-operative framework; communal labour can be included and developed in it. For a desperately poor peasantry needs, above all, a co-operative framework.

To give actual evidence of this poverty I quote two typical family budgets from the Fulani area in Guinea taken from a study by J. Perrin in *Afrique Française*, December 1938.

I. Mamadon Bodio Sow, aged 40, married, one son aged 14; small cultivator in the *marga* of Soumbaraboutout, Kiniampili village, Kaba Canton, 45 km. from the railway. Information collected in 1937.

A. RECEIPTS. Harvest for the year 1936–7

Rice	400 kg. @ 1 fr. 50	fr. 600
Fonio	245 kg. @ 1 fr.	245
Millet	—	—
Sweet potatoes (dried)	105 kg. @ 0 fr. 40	42
Maize	50 kg. @ 0 fr. 30	15
Groundnuts	20 kg. @ 0 fr. 75	15
Squash	20 kg. @ 1 fr.	20
Cotton	10 kg. @ 1 fr.	10
Indigo (collected)		25
Shea butter	70 kg. @ 0 fr. 75	52.50
Sesame	10 kg. @ 0 fr. 50	5
Wax (2 hives)	2 kg.	15
Honey	18 litres	25
Livestock: 2 cows, 1 heifer, increase 2 calves		100
	Total	1169.50

128 FREEDOM AND AUTHORITY IN FRENCH WEST AFRICA

B. EXPENSES

Food:

Rice	300 kg. @ 1 fr. 50	450
Sweet potatoes	105 kg. @ 0 fr. 40	42
Maize	45 kg. @ 0 fr. 30	13.50
Groundnuts	25 kg. @ 0 fr. 75	18.75
Squash		20

Seed. Loan from Provident Society:

Rice	80 kg.
Fonio	33 kg.
Millet	1 kg.
Groundnuts	20 kg.

Clothes:

1 boubou (outer garment) weaving	fr. 15	
cotton (spun by wife), dyeing (by wife)	10	
20 measures of rice	20	
	—	45
1 pr. cotton trousers		5
Cotton cap		5
1 veil for wife		15
1 cotton drape for wife		20
1 kerchief		5
1 slip for daughter		5
1 cotton cloth boubou		5

Guests passing through:

Rice	150 kg. @ 1 fr. 50	225
Broad beans	50 kg. @ 1 fr. 50	75
Helper for the hut		15
Helper for the field		15
Helper for palm-oil collection		10
Salt	5 kg.	15

Utensils:

1 enamel bowl	20
3 calabashes	15
Canari	3
3 hoes	7.50
Axe	3
Cooking pot	10
Hives—3 for	1
Soap	4
Umbrella	12.50
3 mats	7.50

Tax	40

Total 1,127.75

C. Receipts: Fr. 1,169.50. *Expenses:* Fr. 1,127.75. *Balance:* 41.75.

THE PEASANT COMMUNITY

II. Karimou Sakamoko, aged 40, former soldier. Three wives, three children aged 7, 5, 5; works with his wives. Malinke—free man—nephew of the Chief of Sakanokala, Houré Canton, 100 km. from Mamou, no road. Belongs to a nucleus of free Malinke who came to the Fouta with the seventeenth-century invasion. Information collected July 1937.

A. RECEIPTS. Harvest, 1936–7.

Rice	1,200 kg. @ 1 fr. 50	fr. 1,800
Fonio—harvest destroyed		
by locusts	35 kg. @ 1 fr.	35
Millet	90 kg. @ 0 fr. 60	54
Maize	150 kg. @ 0 fr. 30	45
Cassava (fresh)	200 kg. @ 0 fr. 25	50
Sweet potatoes	200 kg. @ 0 fr. 40	80
Groundnuts	20 kg. @ 0 fr. 75	15
Bananas	1,000 kg. @ 0 fr. 15	150
Cotton	10 kg. @ 1 fr.	10
Pepper	about 10 kg.	14
Indigo		45
Livestock: 4 cows, increase 2 calves		100
6 chickens @ 2 fr. 50		15
	Total	2,413

Coilected products, wild yams and fruits eaten in the dry season, cannot be assessed but eke out harvested food.

B. EXPENSES

Food, including exchanges, travellers, visitors:

Rice	760 kg. @ 1 fr. 50	fr. 1,140
Fonio	17 kg. @ 1 fr.	17
Millet	50 kg. @ 0 fr. 60	3C
Cassava	200 kg. @ 0 fr. 25	50
Sweet potatoes	200 kg. @ 0 fr. 40	80
Bananas	1,000 kg. @ 0 fr. 15	150
Groundnuts	15 kg. @ 0 fr. 75	11.25
Maize	150 kg. @ 0 fr. 30	45
Palm-oil	1 tin (18 kg.)	50
Salt	25 kg.	70

Cultivation (seed):

Rice	120 kg. @ 1 fr. 50	180
Fonio	17 kg. @ 1 fr.	17
Millet	2 kg. 500 @ 0 fr. 60	1.50
Maize	2 kg. @ 0 fr. 30	0.60

Food of helpers (1 day):

Rice	15 kg. @ 1 fr. 50	fr. 22.50
Chicken	5 @ 2 fr. 50	12.50

130 FREEDOM AND AUTHORITY IN FRENCH WEST AFRICA

Groundnuts	4 kg. @ 0 fr. 75	3	
Kola nuts		15	
		—	53

Present to the singing-man:

Cash	20	
Salt	2	
Palm-oil	10	
	—	32

Purchase of livestock:

A two-year-old heifer for		
4 baskets of rice, say	160 kg. @ 1 fr. 50	240

Clothes (for the head of the family):

1 boubou	fr.	70
1 pr. trousers		20
Cap		15
Shirt		17.50
Piece of calico		30
Making of the boubou		5
Blanket		27.50
Slippers		8

Clothes (for the women):

3 slips @ 17.50	52.50
3 kerchiefs	23.50
3 cotton drapes	62.50

Clothes (for the children):

3 blouses	15
3 packets of blue balls	3.75

Utensils:

Soap	5	
1 trunk	42.50	
Umbrella	12.50	
5 mats	12.50	
2 hatchets	5.50	
4 hoes	12	
3 basins	73.50	
3 small bowls	18	
Axe	3	
Cooking pot	17.50	
3 dishes	9	
Hurricane lamp	11.50	
Paraffin	15	
	—	587.75

Taxes		80
Sundries:		
Expenses of travelling to Mamou (3 trips a year)		50
Sent to Mamou for sundry purposes		20
Sundry presents		60
Purchase of kola nuts		15

THE PEASANT COMMUNITY

House (square of four huts, one rebuilt each year):

1 door	fr. 12.50	
Walls	25	
Stakes	5	
Covering	7.50	
Food for workmen	7	
	—	57
Purchase of 20 seccos (mats of thick straw)		60
Covering for another hut		11.50
	Total expenses	3,108.60

C. *Balance:* Receipts—fr. 2,413. Expenses—fr. 3,108.60. Balance —695.60.

This result does not correspond to the kind of life led by the subject. This family is obviously well off, and the estimate of income is not exact, while that of expenditure is. Throughout this region, gold deposits discovered at that time were being worked, but this source of profit could not be declared, as working was forbidden.

In Morocco, it appears from studies made by Réné Hoffherr and Roger Morris, that the resources of the small peasant are similar to those indicated in these family budgets (*Revenues et niveaux de vie indigènes au Maroc,* Receuil Sirey, 1934).

Thus for this population of poor peasants, where the circulation of money is almost negligible, and where the traditional structure has already been broken, a new institution is required which can acquire new forms of wealth and build up a new social structure. And in relation to a metropolitan economy, buttressed with owners' cartels and workers' trade unions, the colony needs an organization which will create an equilibrium and control the peasant producers of raw materials for the cartels and syndicates.

In the Provident Societies which are taking shape and gathering strength under the tutelage of the *Cercle* Commandants, I see the germ of a native co-operative organization. I personally would like the co-operative to specialize in one product. The prosperity of agricultural co-operatives rests on specialization. The corporate group of cultivators will come to life if all its members are united to produce and care for a single crop. Their professional homogeneity will be safeguarded and their community spirit fostered if they are concerned with one product only. If they are associated in a Provident Society for the cultivation of groundnuts, while individually free to produce rice, millet, fonio, eggs or chickens, they will have the advantage of a common discipline without being confined within too rigid a framework.

132 FREEDOM AND AUTHORITY IN FRENCH WEST AFRICA

It is essential, however, to choose the right product. It must be one which can pass beyond the native section into the colonial section of the national economy. Let us examine the process, for there is none which it is more important to direct carefully, both for the territorial administration and for native policy in general. It is a sort of lock-gates, where the product is passed from one economic level to another. At this lock-gate the peasant undergoes a *loss of strength;* sometimes he has a five days' walk to the trading store, carrying in baskets the goods to fill the lorries. When he is paid, he suffers a *loss of exchange;* the notes or cash which he receives have not the same purchasing power within the native economy to which he will return as cowries or the old silver coinage. A shrewd Commandant knows these things and recognizes that they are not negligible. It is obvious that the peasant will be at a grave disadvantage if he is left to himself to convey his crop from the native to the colonial section. Equally obvious are the benefits rendered by a collective sales organization such as the Provident Society provides. One can foresee in the near future agreements being made between Provident Societies and European business and commercial firms, on some such lines as these:

Native Provident Societies, having been legally empowered to organize the sale of commodities produced by their members, the N.P.S. of X District solicits the co-operation of Z Company:

1. In virtue of its competence to supply a given product of the required quality.

2. In virtue of its competence to ensure the sale of a given product on the world market.

A contract will then be signed between the Company and the N.P.S. defining the reciprocal obligations of the contracting parties.

Such a contract, subject to the approval of the Governor General, and if its results were satisfactory, might well be extended to all the districts concerned with the product in question. A protocol should then be added defining the obligations of the Company towards the different Societies in regard to future arrangements concerning the same product.

What would be the practical application of such agreements?

i. *Organization of markets*

The commercial company, being a specialized enterprise, would undertake the 'finishing' of commodities purchased from the N.P.S.,

THE PEASANT COMMUNITY 133

thus ensuring a better quality than unspecialized middlemen or the Societies themselves could achieve.

The Company would organize purchasing centres in the district at which lorries would call at regular fixed times and collect the whole stock. A representative of the Provident Society would be present, at least in the initial stages. Members of the Society would agree to suspend production temporarily at the request of the Company, thus avoiding over-production. Payments would of course be made on the spot.

ii. *Elimination of middle-men*

Prices would be fixed in relation to world prices, either by studying the figures of previous years or by analysing and examining the difference between world prices and local prices (the difference should provide interest on capital and cover against risk), or by a combination of the two methods. Naturally, the establishment of this relationship would require detailed study and the use of every possible source of information, including the Company's own records. The local price should be fixed at a proportion of the average world price for the previous week as quoted by the Company and checked by the Economics Bureau of French West Africa. In this way the price would be fixed automatically, without room for argument, and would be the maximum figure payable by any non-speculative purchaser.

A part of the Company's profits would be refunded to the Provident Society. This clearly makes it necessary for the Company's books to be available for examination by the Administration's Audit Commissioners, and this in turn requires a uniform method of presenting balance sheets and the standardization of the rules for calculating profits obtaining at the time of the signing of the contract.

iii. *Stabilization of prices*

Profits refunded to the native Provident Society would be paid into a special compensation fund to be used for subsidizing purchase prices in periods of slump. Subsidies should never be applied on such a scale as to increase the purchase price beyond the maximum prices obtaining, for example, during the previous three years. This point is naturally of more particular interest to the Society, but the stabilization of producers' remuneration is not without importance for the Company also.

134 FREEDOM AND AUTHORITY IN FRENCH WEST AFRICA

iv. *New Activities*

The total utilization of the product is only possible if adequate amounts are offered for sale, but the organization of purchasing centres sufficiently near together should enable this to be done. As regards production for export to the metropolitan country, where a considerable demand exists, it should be possible to require the Company (*a*) to maintain a sufficient number of European and African agents to direct native cultivation of new crops; (*b*) to accept trainees on plantations, both Government demonstrators and voluntary native planters.

It is obvious that co-operation between the Department of Agriculture and the Company will be essential as much in the selection of crops and their distribution as in the education of the natives.

v. *Continuity of aims and intentions*

This continuity, which the Administration only too often lacks, is exactly what the Company would provide. It is clearly in the interests of the Company that the marketing of the product should be organized under its direction, and that its own activities should be extended to other fields. The world market is unstable, the metropolitan market is less so. It would seem that in the circumstances the interests of the Company and of the producers will coincide. Directors of companies are no doubt actuated by the best intentions, but changes of personnel have to be reckoned with, and the strongest of bonds is a clearly recognized mutual interest.

A number of objections have been raised to these projects. I shall proceed to examine the most important of them:

1. The Native Provident Society cannot compel its members to sell their produce to the Company. Pressure has been applied in the past in many a colony on behalf of private interests; it is surely quite legitimate to-day to use propaganda for purposes of public interest among natives completely ignorant of economic affairs.

2. The remuneration of some producers is inadequate. If one starts with a predetermined scale of remuneration, one may arrive at a price which is incompatible with the requirements of the world market. Predetermined prices or standards of living on the one hand, and free competition and world markets on the other are mutually antagonistic. If, however, by effective organization, the market for a product can be controlled, it will be possible to balance the low prices at certain periods by the high prices at other periods, as already des-

THE PEASANT COMMUNITY   135

cribed. But at the same time other opportunities will be explored, and
also efforts will be made to capture the protected metropolitan market, which will lend itself more readily to the opening of new channels
of trade and thus to the fixing of a standard of living.

3. Pressure on the natives and forced labour. There would be no
question of applying the smallest degree of compulsion to increase
native production or extend cultivation. But respect for the liberty
of the individual need not inhibit all propaganda, nor prevent the
giving of instruction for fear of influencing free decision. Moreover,
it is absolutely necessary to take into account and to make use of the
social organization of the various communities, otherwise one condemns oneself to complete impotence. The very necessary and desir-
able progress in this field cannot come to pass all in a moment.

4. Manœuvres on the part of the Trading Company. Any undesir-
able manœuvres on the part of the Trading Company can easily be
checked if its operations are followed closely enough, through
auditors, examination of books, etc. There are, of course, numerous
details which would have to be studied and regulated.

Provision could be made for contracts to be annulled, in particular
if fraud could be proved. Moreover, in regard to complementary
activities, contracts could be terminable at ten years with the option
of renewal if no serious difficulties had arisen in their execution and
if results were satisfactory.

Nowadays, it seems, lack of organization is universally condemned, and more especially in the field of competition in the world
markets. The type of contract I have described is designed precisely
to produce organization, to prepare for the future, and not to be
attached to any particular system.

3. *Education: the rural adult school.* In order to be re-established in
its own Africa, and to be organized as to production and marketing,
the peasant community must be educated. The Commandant, with
the Council of Elders, should lay down a regional scheme for an
agreed plan of production. The execution of the plan should be under
the direction of teams of African demonstrators trained in an agricultural school. Family or individual plantations should be laid out,
almost adjoining, to facilitate direction by the teams and control by
agricultural engineers.

But the real education will be given in schools of a new type and
with a new purpose: people's rural schools. Instead of skimming the
cream of the villages for young people to fill the native grades in the
Administration, the villages themselves will be put to school to learn

136 FREEDOM AND AUTHORITY IN FRENCH WEST AFRICA

a new way of African life. Schools for millet-growers, schools for cocoa-planters will reflect the individual character of the area in which each one is situated. French will be learned in a concrete and practical way, by means of peasant tools, by groups of pupils using the tools, working in an experimental field and teaching one another. Inspector General Charton, who founded these rural schools, also opened a training school for native teachers. Success has been achieved, and a whole peasant world seems to have found again the consciousness of their country and their labour.

4. *Giving the peasant community a political expression.* Finally the peasant community must be represented politically in the conduct of affairs. There must be in the colony, in the province and at the base, in the village itself, councils of workers, who one day will vote and control taxation. But these councils, though necessary, are not enough. There must be a chief. We come back to the question of the village chief. An official cannot represent the peasantry, neither can a landlord. The peasant community will choose its chiefs and constitute its councils within the sphere in which it is beginning to be active: the people's rural schools and the producers' co-operative.

A peasant class is being built up in West Africa adjoining and buttressing Berber Africa. The former victims of forced labour are coming to realize what voluntary labour is. Recognized as true peasants, they are now organized and ready for a real federation with Metropolitan France, and this would appear to be the natural course of events. But there is still need for a native policy, carried out on the spot by territorial administrators and understood and supported by the mother country.

THOUSANDS OF VILLAGES ARE WAITING

This is the policy required for the African peasant community, a native policy in every sense of the term. It is not the result of a superficial sentimentality; it does not wallow in romantic ideas about the peasantry; it registers a fact of human geography peculiar to West Africa: in a country where the highest density of the rural population only reaches thirty-five per square kilometre and averages between ten and twenty, where the greater part of the agricultural products are of poor quality, the peasant community is the only organization capable of re-creating an indigenous social life and effecting the necessary equilibrium between the life of the colony and that of the native territories.

THE PEASANT COMMUNITY

A peasant policy is not a weapon for use against the European colony. If it does oppose the waste of manpower in forced labour and on plantations as well as the disproportionate amounts allocated from the budgets to privileged concerns, such as the Niger Office,[1] it does so in the interests of the general public and in order to raise the African standard of life. The troubles of the European colony at present arise from the fact that the standard of living among the natives is too low. M. Paul Reynard has offered a striking comparison: The metropolitan country is a ship to which a small boat, the colony, is attached. But the ship rides higher in the water than the small boat does. To fling numbers of European colonists into Africa is to throw more weight into the little boat, causing it to capsize and break its moorings. What ought to be done is to raise the water level, that is, the economic level, and this can be done by developing the peasantry. Far from injuring the colony, a well-established peasantry will be its best support. At present the colonists are trying without success to expand and take over isolated ill-equipped villages; they try to fill up the cracks by starting new crops, which they have in the end to leave to the natives because they produce them more cheaply. These same villages, equipped and reconstituted, might well be a centre for European enterprise.

A peasant policy, while arousing the powers of renewal natural to Africa, does not mean an effortless and dangerous domination. It will force us to reconsider many administrative problems, and in the first place to solve the problem of local councils and their relation to the colonial government. It will force us to purify and perfect the exercise of authority and to turn our backs on the caricature of authority displayed by totalitarian states in Europe. Finally, such a policy is in the French tradition. It invites the peasant household to become a landed proprietor; it will restore to African life that element which the proletariat of the plantations lacked: the delight of living by work done on one's own land for oneself. Such a peasant policy cannot possibly destroy the sovereignty of France because it will spread abroad in Africa the typical French culture—that of a nation of gardeners.

This policy does not aim at making every African a peasant. Neither does it plan to concentrate them artificially in certain well-advertised areas which will have to be constructed at great expense from the

---

[1] Translator's note: A self-contained administrative enterprise which was intended to transform the Niger Valley into a cotton-growing area, similar to the Gezira experiment in the Anglo-Egyptian Soudan.

138 FREEDOM AND AUTHORITY IN FRENCH WEST AFRICA

foundations. It is simply designed to help those who are already peasants to a better way of life and to help them in their own homes and in their own country.

Out of 48,000 villages, half are already easily accessible, being within reach of a permanent system of communications, road or railway, which their own labour has helped to build. Now they are waiting for the road or the railway to help them by equipping them with wells, stores, small tools, the many important small things which go to make up rural civilization. Through the unseen efforts of the territorial administration, through the personal devotion of unknown Commandants, the African village has won legal recognition in the colony itself. According to whether the Metropolitan Government recognizes the village or abandons it the Union will stand or fall.

IX. THE NEW AFRICAN WORLD

Two hundred and fifty years ago, an African lived at the Court of King Louis XIV. His name was Anabia[1] and he was the son of the king of Issiny. The kingdom of Issiny has left no great memories in Africa; to-day all that remains of it is the small maritime town of Assinie in the Ivory Coast. But European travellers in those days naturally gave royal honours to any African ruler; when a Frenchman, the Chevalier d'Amon, crossed the bar and landed in Issiny, he paid his respects to the ruler of the country as he would have done to a king, and when he returned to France he took Anabia, the king's young son, with him. He found a lodging for him at first in the house of a dealer in pearls in the Rue Tiquetonne, who no doubt financed trading companies on the Slave Coast. The Chevalier introduced his protégé to Madame de Maintenon. Louis saw Anabia and put him under the care of Bossuet to be instructed in the Christian faith; the king stood godfather to him at his baptism, gave him the rank of an officer and settled on him an income sufficient for him to live like a gentleman of fashion. Meanwhile, back in Africa the king of Issiny died and Anabia was at once treated as the heir to that far-away throne. He immediately founded an Order of Chivalry, The Star of Notre Dame, for which he secured the blessing of the Cardinal de Noailles, and straightway went off to occupy his throne, leaving the Ministry of Marine to pay his debts. It is recorded that when he took leave of the king, Louis said to him: 'Prince Anabia, the only difference between us now is the difference between black and white.'

In those days, Europe knew nothing of Africa except the coastal regions, and sought there trading stations rather than territories. Europeans did not look for peasants to be established on their own land, but for slaves to be transported to the islands. It was not till the nineteenth century that the revelation and liberation of the Dark Continent began. To-day a new African world is arising. The African kings who still survive have the status of protected rulers, but the Africa of the villages is struggling to bring new chiefs to birth while

[1] The story of Anabia was published by Paul Roussier, keeper of the records in the Ministry of Colonies: *L'Établissement d'Issiny*, Librairie Larose, 1935.

140 FREEDOM AND AUTHORITY IN FRENCH WEST AFRICA

yesterday's overlords are the government officials of to-morrow. The European legal code has broken native custom, but custom is being reborn to express itself in Law. Slaves and serfs are rising up as the colonists of their own soil. Directed, organized, armed for production, they are about to come of age economically and to re-establish a solid peasant community. In this new African world, where we have been able to distinguish the elements of a threefold evolution, political, juridical and agrarian, King Louis' words to Anabia seem to echo with the very accent of to-day, to assert the real meaning of the evolution of Africa.

When Louis XIV said to Anabia 'The only difference between us now is the difference between black and white' he was emphasizing the fact that they were both kings, jointly participating in royalty, and that while they differed in colour, they were one by virtue of their royal nature. To-day it is a question of an identity of civilization between Africa and Europe.

In 1934 I revisited Dakar, now a town of 60,000 Africans and 10,000 Europeans, the capital of an empire and a great sea and airport. I visited the Native Medical School and chatted with the students. Of the 50,000 pupils in the schools of French West Africa, fifty young men have been selected for training as doctors. They are drawn from all the colonies, all the ethnic groups of the vast Federation: from the Soudan, from Dahomey, from the Wolof of Senegal, the Apollonians of the Ivory Coast. They feel themselves to be citizens of a new Africa, working to protect its health. We agree, they and I, that they have a great part to play and that they ought to devote themselves to public health work rather than to the acquisition of a small 'educated' clientele. I hope that they will function in their corner of Africa as did Balzac's country doctor who civilized a corner of Savoy.

'To be a man of good will', said the country doctor, 'is not enough. To civilize the most insignificant corner of the earth, it is necessary to be educated; but education, integrity and patriotism in themselves are nothing without a firm determination to sacrifice all personal advantage and dedicate oneself to serving the community.'

The service which the African doctor can offer to the community will be to do his share of the total of four million consultations a year; to organize and conduct crusades against epidemics and infant mortality; to take part in the battle against plague, leprosy, sleeping sickness, infantile diarrhoea, and the injurious practices of midwives.

We are in Africa, in the African sphere of medicine. But suddenly one of these young students puts a question which reminds me of

THE NEW AFRICAN WORLD 141

Louis XIV's words to Anabia. 'What do they think of us in Paris?' he asks. We should realize what this question means. 'We are young West Africans, students of the Native Medical School of Dakar. What do they think about us in Paris? We want to know what they think in order, first, to show that we exist, in order to assert our personality and to be sure that we are recognized as doctors not only in Dakar but in Paris. And we hope that some great doctor in Paris will reply to us in the royal words: "The only difference between you and me is the difference between black and white." We are doctors just as white men are; we have a particular job as doctors, a job to do for African society but not in a subordinate rank.'

This is something quite new in the relationship between a European mother country and its native colony. The new African world is aiming at making Europe revise its ideas about Africa. The forms and the aims of African work have changed owing to the intervention and the influence of Europe. And Africa itself is aware of the change.

West Africa is becoming a section of the modern world, just as Europe is. The plane which links Paris to Dakar in less than thirty hours finds at the airport of Ouahkam the same kind of airfield as Le Bourget. The cranes at the docks, whether African or European, look like gigantic sea-horses. The same diadem of electric lights glitters at night on the brow of the town, whether the town is white or black. The same radio blares the world's news to the Senegalese jeweller and to his fellow in Paris.

Groundnuts, cocoa, bananas and mahogany are dependent on the world market in the same way as wheat, wine, preserves and steel. And in Africa as in Europe prices, salaries and living standards may be regulated by the American Stock Exchange. A liner leaving Dakar harbour carries pilgrims bound for Mecca as well as troops for Djibouti; West Africa is part of the Moslem community and these pilgrims will foregather with Indian pilgrims. It is also one of the federated provinces of the Union Française and its troops perform military duties for the other colonies and, if need be, for Metropolitan France. Another liner, arriving, brings missionaries for a Christian Africa which is growing up as a province of the Catholic Church. In the material as in the spiritual sphere Africa is indeed becoming in every sense part of the modern world. On the material plane her equipment, her economy, her power, no longer differentiate her from the rest of the world. On the spiritual plane also she is in communication with Europe. She is not so ready as formerly she was to be subordinated to Europe or to accept an inferior status, and she is waiting

142 FREEDOM AND AUTHORITY IN FRENCH WEST AFRICA

to hear Europe proclaim: 'The only difference between us now is the difference between black and white.'

There is another element which is quite new, and which operates not between Africa and Europe but within African social life, between the development of modern Africa and the persistence of the Africa of the past. Africa is conscious of change not merely in her relations with Europe; she is aware of a conflict of generations within herself.

At the Native Medical School in Dakar a student in the dissecting-room is performing an autopsy. He is endeavouring to discover scientifically the cause of death. What could be more natural? But, for an enormous proportion of Africa, which still belongs to the past and regards death as due to the action of supernatural powers, what could be more revolutionary? The medical student who is performing the autopsy comes from a district of the Ivory Coast where, formerly, the dead man would have been carried through the village amid demonstrations of mass delirium. Diviners, guardians of the ancestral cult, would have called on the spirit of the dead man, adjuring him to name the agent responsible for his death. To-day in modern Africa, magic has been replaced by the autopsy, and our medical student has under his hands not only the dead body of a man, but the corpse of an ancient custom and the birth of a new world.

As he works I see in my mind's eye his father who has come to Dakar to take part in the Government Council. The father is a powerful and wealthy chief in the cocoa country, where the money to be made in the cocoa industry is giving rise to a new African middle class; in his clothing and personal appearance the old and the new Africa are mingled. He wears European shoes with a flowing native robe; gold-stopped teeth and tribal scarifications; visible sock-suspenders and invisible amulets. In imagination I set him over against his son, austerely dressed in his white surgeon's gown, and I wonder whether the difference between father and son is not greater than that between the son and us—not a difference of colour but, within the one Africa, the difference in outlook between an old world and a new.

So the question which has to be asked is, whether we can govern the son in the same way and by the same methods with which we have governed the father. Will the son, when one day he takes his seat in the Council, bring to it the same mind as his father did? Will not our native policy have to change if it is to go on at all? And in the meantime we have to reckon already with the latent conflict between the new world and the old.

Here is another student, not the son of a notable but of a humble

THE NEW AFRICAN WORLD 143

policeman in the Upper Volta, a district police guard. To give him a little pocket-money while at Dakar, so that he could go dancing on Sundays with the daughters of wealthy tradesmen, his brother went into the Gold Coast to work on a plantation; so the postal orders sent by an illiterate labourer, with the aid of a professional letter-writer, enable a medical student to play the young man about town in the new African world.

This unknown labourer is a symbol of the new Africa just as much as the medical student is. Money has changed him as the medical school has changed the other. Though he is an illiterate labourer he has been fitted into a mechanism which has nothing in common with the old colonial economy. Without being aware of it he is operating a system of production in which four factors are involved: a local factor, which is the Gold Coast plantation where he earns his money; an inter-colonial factor, because he has moved from the French Colony of the Ivory Coast into the British Colony of the Gold Coast; a metropolitan factor, since his labour concerns two metropolitan countries; finally a world factor, in the form of a bar of chocolate. But he does not see as far as that; he is merely devoted to his brother.

When the medical student returns to his own village he will be keenly aware of a number of differences. The elders will treat him with a sort of defiant deference mixed with a slightly ironic resentment. He wears a uniform, he is an official and he exercises, to some extent, the powers of the Administration. But they make fun of his little box of books, and the way he behaves. They ask his mother whether, since he knows so much, he still knows how to eat porridge from a calabash and how to sleep on a mat in a hut. When he confides all this to me, I ask him: 'Do you at least go and pay your respects to the Chief?' to which he straightway replies: 'I can't do that any more.' Now I know that area and the chief; it is the Mossi country and the chief is a Naba. For more than eight hundred years the Naba has been the political and territorial ruler, the father and the judge of his people, and there is a customary ritual for doing obeisance to him; the people prostrate themselves before him and hit the ground with their elbows, lifting up their hands and bowing their heads so that their foreheads are smeared with dust. This ritual salutation is called *poussi*. My young man was quite willing to greet the chief in the European way, but, said he, 'I cannot do *poussi*.'

It seemed simple enough in Dakar, but out there, in his own village, the old Africa is still powerful. On a track which leads from the village the Naba appears: an old man on horseback, his big toe gripped in a

144 FREEDOM AND AUTHORITY IN FRENCH WEST AFRICA

rope stirrup; at his horse's tail runs a servant, the *sorone*, who carries on his shoulder a nail-studded club. The medical student goes to meet the Naba who awaits the customary *poussi*, for a salutation in European style from a native is no proper greeting. If the Naba does not receive the traditional *poussi*, he will not understand why, but will think that the French have betrayed him by taking this young man away from the village and perverting him. And in practice the opinion of the chief will have considerable importance for native policy. He will cause it to be rumoured in the villages that the schools in Dakar turn the young men's heads and that the Commandant no longer works hand in hand with the elders and the old chiefs. Moreover, in matters of health, instead of helping the young doctor to overcome the ingrained habits of the village he will hinder him and frustrate his efforts. Then the health question will become a political matter, and the Commandant will need all the tact of which he is capable to reconcile the young doctor and the old chief. This can only be done by the Commandant and by one who knows his job.

Thus it is not enough to train African doctors; it is also necessary to get them accepted by their own people; it is not enough to create a new African world; it is also necessary to graft it on to the old Africa without causing upheavals. And far from being superseded by an evolutionary progress towards self-sufficiency, a native policy and a territorial administration are more necessary than ever in this Africa which is conscious of having become different from what it was. But native policy must proceed by securing harmony, not by issuing orders, and administration will consist more and more in arbitrating between older and younger generations. It may be thought that these are special cases, which are still rare and only affect the 'intellectuals'. But the masses also are progressing. Let us consider more closely the African village where we have seen our young doctor at work. In just such a village, when a matter of health was in question, I observed a fact of social significance: the village was divided into wards, and each ward was the domain of one family. Near each ward was a waterhole, a little pool from which the family drew its drinking water. A ward always implied the existence and the use of such a waterhole. Now all the families suffered from the same complaint, the guinea worm, caused by the water in the pools. We wanted to change this, and the only way to do so was to get drinking-water from a well instead of from pools. We couldn't sink a well for each ward, so we made one common well for them all. But the families wouldn't use it, not because it was too far away, but because

THE NEW AFRICAN WORLD
145

it was for all of them; it was no longer their own private water supply.

At that time the country was undergoing a very profound change. The young men were earning money as a result of new crops and new trade, and having money they could pay bride-price and get married. Moreover, instead of living in the ward with their families and adding one more hut to the homestead, they built themselves independent homes, one for each couple, placed round the well, which became the focus of attraction, the vital centre of a new village. A very new village, in fact, concentrated not dispersed, consisting of households which had detached themselves from their families and were becoming a city in embryo. The notion of a city, it seems, has taken root there as one of the acquisitions of the new Africa.

There is, finally, a third new element, complementary to the other two and more surprising. Africa is becoming a section of the modern world, both in relation to Europe and in relation to the old African world, and a section with its own individual character. If Europe said to Africa: 'There is now no difference between you and me except the difference between black and white,' Africa would acquiesce, but would emphasize with particular pride the significance of that very difference. The Africa of our day is proud to be linked with Europe, and to be in many respects like Europe; but at the same time it takes pride in its own African personality. The Africa of to-day is shaking off the yoke of the old Africa, in which nevertheless the sources of its individuality are to be found.

The racial problem, for example, no longer operates in one direction only. There are educated Africans now who are proud of their colour and who feel within themselves a growing African patriotism. With passionate interest they delve into the legends and poetry of the past and study the surviving remains of the pre-colonial, pre-slave-trade and pre-Moslem Africa. The student-teachers of Gorée, at their speech-days, are no longer content to act the plays of Molière and Labiche. They stage, in French, dramas based on old Dahomean or Soudanese themes. And some of the intellectuals are beginning to think: 'We may borrow from Europe the means of expression, but we turn for inspiration to our own Africa.' I believe I detected such a state of mind in an African priest, when he was speaking of his pagan childhood. On embracing Christianity he had not been converted from simple superstition, but from another religion. He considered that fetishism fell short of the truth but was not without a richness of its own. It was indeed a religion which possessed mysteries,

146 FREEDOM AND AUTHORITY IN FRENCH WEST AFRICA

worship, a priesthood, convents and a mysticism peculiar to itself. And he, the convert, profoundly Christian and profoundly a priest, recognized the religions of his country as error in relation to the Cross but not as African inferiority in relation to Europe.

A new African world exists which we have called into being and which our native policy has brought to birth. I do not believe that this birth has occurred only in French West Africa. New Africas are being born in Sierra Leone, in the Gold Coast, in Nigeria and Angola and the Belgian Congo, and they all have features in common.

Belgians, Portuguese, British, French are all at work there, each with his own national temperament, and each nation's native policy reflects its own particular genius. Nevertheless the results are comparable. Confronted by the realities of Africa each has devised methods more or less similar. Whether chiefs, judges or peasants are concerned, we have all in our different ways succeeded in calling into being the New African World. And this result has been achieved, not by means of an ideology, but by trial and error. This new world is not a theoretical construction but a living reality, the fruit of an experimental native policy. It does indeed exist, and it presents us with a supremely important question: shall we continue to inspire its progress or shall we leave it to itself? It is a matter of life or death for Africa as well as for us.

To those in Europe who would deny us the right to carry on our work for Africa we can reply with confidence. Our methods have justified themselves; we have powerfully renewed Africa; we are renewing her native chiefs, her customary law, her peasants, and in doing so we are revealing her to the world and to herself. On what ideological grounds is it proposed to put a stop to this experiment? What so-called realism can ignore our actual achievement?

And to those in Africa who, inflamed by racial pride, would deny us the right to administer colonies, we could give the same answer: Beware of racialism, among Blacks or Whites. It is capable of rousing the Africans, in Africa itself, against French universalism. Universalism is regarded as a form of intellectual cross-breeding which corrupts the mind as physical cross-breeding corrupts the blood; the mind can only develop if the blood is pure; there is a Negro mind as there is an Aryan mind and each should be reared in its own 'zoo'. There is no natural identity between the Negro and the Aryan mind: neither humanism nor Christianity can reduce their differences, and any intercourse between them would defile both and engender only a monstrous growth. The mind is the supreme expression of racial

THE NEW AFRICAN WORLD 147

consciousness; the influence of a culture can only be spread in so far as it is sub-cultural. Such is the strange regeneration preached to the African world by those new champions, who, professing to honour the tribal gods, act the slave trader on their own soil.

But we also seek to preserve African cultures; we also would restore the African to himself, but so that we may at the same time restore to him the dignity of human personality. And this is where the spirit of peace resides.

Governor General van Vollenhoven had already realized, before he was killed in action at Villers-Cotteret in 1918, that the true destiny of Africa lay not in a chequer-board of self-contained colonies but in an inter-colonial co-operation in which the metropolitan countries also were partners, and in which the conception of trusteeship should replace that of exploitation.

The metropolitan country is not the sole proprietor of the colony, neither is the colony a 'possession'; it belongs as much to the native territories as to the metropolis, or rather it issues from the native territories. It is a new world which subsists by exchanges and can lead the metropolis no less than the native territories towards co-operation with other native and metropolitan countries.

It is in the light of these considerations that the plan which Vollen-hoven offered to the European nations should be understood. He wished them to be organized against a new German pressure. There was no question of establishing in Africa a sort of international authority under which the sovereignty—and the responsibility—of the Colonial Powers would quickly vanish; nor of protecting, by the form of a limited company, the operations of a group of financiers who, under the pretext of redistributing primary products, would serve the interests of monopolists. But it is vitally necessary that neighbouring Colonial Powers, who have had long experience and are already partners in fact and in spirit in the native territories which they govern, should co-operate actively in a programme of large-scale public works and small-scale rural development, in a customs and monetary union and in an intercolonial system of African law. Conditions are the more favourable since a common basis of policy already exists in the African peasant community, in which the four nations interested in West Africa—Britain, Belgium, Portugal and France—are in agreement.

The concluding words of my account of the new African world are addressed to Leopold Sedar Senghor, for we are both, in our in-dividual persons, involved in it. My feelings sometimes impel and

148 FREEDOM AND AUTHORITY IN FRENCH WEST AFRICA

sometimes restrain me, and I would hesitate to invoke him were it not that in the face of what threatens us, we must assert our common right to live—he the black man and I the white—in freedom and as comrades. What threatens us? The racialism of to-day, more enervating to the spirit than the most exhausting African climate is to anaemic Europeans.

Leopold Sedar Senghor is not an abstraction. He has a life of his own which began in a particular corner of the world. He was born in that district of Senegal which is known as the 'Little Coast', of a family of Serer shop-keepers. His home town, Joal, was once a Portuguese trading station, where there may still be seen old stone houses, most rare in this country of sandy wastes and native huts, but now without European inhabitants except for a Customs officer and a priest. Some few miles from the now deserted coast, at the edge of the salt pans which glitter like frost under the leaden tropical sky, stretches the new trade route, the estuary of the Saloum. He could have observed there a scene drawn with geometrical precision: a cargo boat lying beside a corrugated shed full of groundnuts. Europe comes there for African fats. He left his native country to take up a scholarship and to become the first *agrégé* from French West Africa in the University of Paris. He is teaching French in a Paris high school while I instruct colonial probationers about Africa. This fact is not merely a figure in the administrative dance, a changing of places within the Union. It is an encounter which horrifies the despots. I am not citing him as a picked specimen, in justification of our colonial methods. His fellows, equally worthy, are still illiterate, living on their own land or on the roads earning their tax money. If colonization has produced schools—which may well be the best things it has produced—they have not always been an unmixed good for the illiterates who have paid for them. In drawing attention to Leopold Senghor I am not trying to justify a system; I don't have to produce him in evidence, for he is not a product of anything—he is a man.

Senghor's compatriot, Blaise Diagne, also left his native country for the colony, and went from the colony to France as the first African deputy, and became Under Secretary of State for the Colonies. But in the course of his career he suffered an increasing loneliness beneath the adulation with which Europeans even more than Africans overwhelmed him. Before he died he told me that there is a sort of corruption, a making things easy, which is more degrading than slavery; and that for us Europeans to yield to an African's pride,

THE NEW AFRICAN WORLD 149

after having satisfied our own, and to honour in him only the *agrégé* or the deputy, was to treat him as less than a man. We are men, and this is the noblest title we can bestow on one another. This title has been disputed and put in doubt by the premiums placed by dictators on bestiality; but in the world-wide struggle, Europe and Africa stand or fall together.

The arena in which Europe and Africa have to defend the same cause has changed for both of us. The fathers of our young Africans were serfs; though the slave trade had been abolished, and Samory had been captured, domestic and agrarian servitude lasted till 1905. The labours of vigilant Commandants, active on tour and in the courts, were needed to make freedom a reality; and then in 1914, when the villages were coming to life again after the inevitable disturbance of social and moral balance consequent on the liberation of the tillers of the soil, came the great famine in the Soudan and the first conscription of troops for the European War. The 175,000 soldiers enrolled during the years 1914–18 dug the grave of the old Africa in the trenches of France and Flanders.

We, too, buried an old Europe beneath the funeral pile of the war. We were not warriors but grave-diggers of worlds. Our young administrators are aware of it. They set out with gold lace on their sleeves, but with a salary in paper money which is less than a workman's wage, when the workman is working for war. They have to step over the bodies of the unemployed to bring into Africa an economic system based on the continued existence of unemployment. In Africa they live in greater comfort than the old explorers ever enjoyed, but they no longer possess that confidence in civilization which the most tattered explorer bore with him like a compass, and they are in danger of losing their way because they are tempted to look backwards—to that old Africa or that old Europe which lies buried under the funeral mound of the war. In vain they try to escape from the Europe which torments them, seeking a refuge in the heart of the Soudan, in an Africa which is no more than a mirage of the desert; or else they think they can still cash in on the prestige of pre-war Europe invested in Africa. But in truth they have not escaped, they cannot live on invested funds, they are pioneers. They do not go to Africa to spread progress (in the words of our elders); they go to Africa to save man's control of progress. This is what we have to defend: you, Senghor in your high school, I in the colonial training college. The physical roads by which you travelled to France and I to French Africa are under fire; the spiritual roads which led to our encounter

150 FREEDOM AND AUTHORITY IN FRENCH WEST AFRICA

are mined; a great fear reigns all about us; we are standing on the foundations of the New Africa as on a beleaguered fortress, fighting the slave traders to preserve our right to be called men.

An African from the Ivory Coast, teaching in Senegal, writes to me: 'Is Europe going to agree to share us out like the first ingathering of the rainy season?' What an apt way of putting it! The first harvest of the rains is the one which provides food for the lean time between harvests, it testifies to the quality of the first sowing and foreshadows the great harvest of the end of the year. The present generation of Africans is the first harvest of the rains; it bridges the gap between the old Africa and the new and is the symbol of the new world.

A delegation of teachers from Gorée were travelling in France. When they were asked what they found most striking, one of them gave this very profound reply: 'The shifting of our own outlook. At home, in the savanna, the eye can see too far; in the forest not far enough. In France one sees everything at the right distance.' It is this rightness of vision which enables us to form a true judgment of those handsome reserves, which are nothing more than prisons. As men we all have a right to this true mental vision.

Such are our comrades of the new African world. Tell them that they can cultivate true judgment without renouncing their savanna and their forests. If I understand them aright, the Africans of to-day do not deny their nature as Africans by adopting that of Frenchmen, nor will they consent to be deprived of either one or the other. Humanism has no meaning unless it leaves them free in their own land to live within its disciplines and to apply the spirit and the methods of the University of Paris to the study of the 'Little Coast' of Senegal. It may be that the colony has no moral right to exist unless it allows these young men to express with their own individual accent the experience they have gained from us as well as from their own country.

I myself would feel shackled, mutilated as a man, if I ceased to be as much aware of that Africa where I have served as of France where I was born, for there is an African element in me now which is in-eradicable. I myself would feel abased if I could not treat you as an equal in Africa as in France. For me humanism consists in our en-counter and our mutual enrichment, and the colony exists morally only if it fosters that humanism which unites us. Together we are entering the new African world and we can say to each other, in the words of the king: 'There is no difference between us except the difference between black and white', a difference which is no longer

THE NEW AFRICAN WORLD

a division or a subordination but a harmony. The essential principle of that harmony seems to me the only thing that can save both France and the new African world, but the practical applications of it have to be thought out afresh, and that is what I have tried to do in this book. I will conclude by summing them up.

We have reached a point where the administrative mind, that is to say, the bureaucratic mind, has lost sight of human beings. It is unable to co-ordinate and harmonize its rigid and fragmentary notions; it lacks courage and loses its grip whenever human necessities encroach on its routine of paper work. Thanks to excessive regulations it has become incapable of independent thought, it is to all intents and purposes already mummified. Faced with a demand for reforms which everyone admits to be necessary it can only propose a re-arrangement of regulations.

What is needed are new methods, so that administration can be born again, vitalized by a spirit of humanism. Whenever a colonial administrator tries to execute plans devised in Paris, he fails. On the other hand, when he acts on his own knowledge of native territories and on his own responsibility, he is successful. This is what governing means, acting not as a specialist but as a humanist, aiming at what is universal in any special case.

That is why I attach so much importance to the native territories in any discussion of colonial affairs. The territory is not just raw material for finance, commerce, army and administration to work with; neither is it something to be made an idol of. It is a living body, and we must enter into relations with it if we are to govern it with full knowledge of what we are doing. Regulations are pinchbeck bureaucratic wares when they no longer answer to the conditions for which they were devised. And these conditions are to be found in the territory itself, not elsewhere; one cannot govern by means of strict regulations any more than by noble sentiments; one can only govern by knowing the country oneself.

And it is necessary to govern. It has been possible to establish producers' co-operatives in French West Africa because there was an effective administration. An African could talk to the Commandant about his groundnuts; what agricultural labourer in France would ring at the Mayor's door to talk to him about his corn?

Effective administration combined with humanity, these are the lines on which action must proceed in order that the new world of Africa may live, in its local chiefs, its provincial institutions, its peasant communities, and so that it may beget men like you, Senghor.

152 FREEDOM AND AUTHORITY IN FRENCH WEST AFRICA

As long as we have Residencies and the means of going on tour, we shall be able to do our job efficiently, to discover the people in their own country, and to serve some purpose other than tyranny. We shall not be corrupted, for we shall always recover, in the Residency and on tour, our sense of brotherhood with the Africans and our own responsibility.

Brotherhood: this is the religion, this the revolution of thought at which a man must arrive if his duties make him responsible for other men and if he wants to preserve his freedom of spirit. 'There is no difference between us now except the difference between black and white.' Is it so hard to imagine brotherhood coexisting with difference?

Even if I were the only person in France who thought these things, our brotherhood would still persist; in this era of menacing racialism, that is my royal pleasure, as former African Commandant and as Frenchman.